3

ACROSS

1 Scorn an offence against the court (8)
5 Orders from the top (6)
9 One may have a chance to clean up here (8)
10 Mother finds a strange gent quite an attraction (6)
12 Valley girl (4)
13 He thinks he knows what's going to happen (10)
15 Happenings in the river now? (7, 6)
19 Back-door methods won't get you in here! (5, 8)
23 It may be used to start something (10)
25 Man to bring back the fruit (4)
28 Sing in a temper (6)
29 Dying for one of the bones in a pile (8)
30 They make the music singable (6)
31 Noel writhing in the grip of outrage (8)

DOWN

1 Metallic blue (6)
2 Birthplace of two small boys (5)
3 He's almost in New York briefly (4)
4 Push to a higher rank? (7)
6 Give the medico a degree of excitement (5)
7 Lady of the lake (9)
8 Day to take tea, we hear, with a girl wit (8)
11 Can't be beaten as a footballer? (4)
14 Make brisk progress when it's wrong to rise (4)
15 He gives out notes from a rich store (9)
16 Head needing to be screwed on properly (3)
17 Source of French wine over the way (4)
18 He has an assured status (8)
20 Observe the money! (4)
21 Ali and Ivor upset by an Italian dish (7)
22 Promise not to drink perhaps (6)
24 Somewhat histrionic style (5)
26 Regret the passing of a little time on a vessel (5)
27 Man of determination (4)

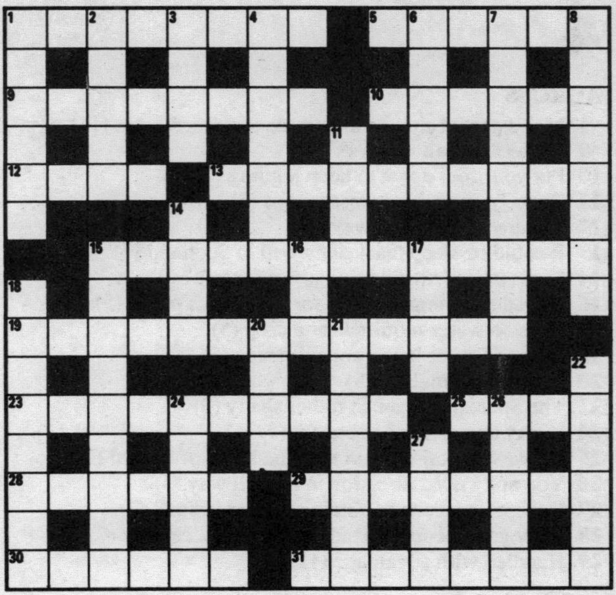
1
2
3
4
5
6
7
8
9
10
11
12
13
14
15
16
17
18
19
20
21
22
23
24
25
26
27
28
29
30
31

4

ACROSS

1 Men's partial change in attitude to subordinates (11)
9 Tickets for sailor-boys? (7)
10 Put your foot down to keep it going (7)
11 Priest brought back in sacrilege (3)
12 Occupy in the usual way (7)
13 It could be sleep that's disturbed in Scotland (7)
14 Some talk of making things hot for you? (3)
15 Hoped to arranged cover for the Jewish priest (5)
17 Note on water required for a crop (5)
18 Fear of Father being not quite nice (5)
20 Luxury bed makers (5)
22 The Spanish lot can be rather shady (3)
24 It may annoy some to burn it (7)
25 Do well as nothing less than the Duke of Milan! (7)
26 You and I need direction in a small way (3)
27 Deceptive means of obtaining clear vision? (7)
28 They go to people's heads on formal occasions (7)
29 Handled with advantage (11)

DOWN

1 Fruity sort of complexion for a girl? Entirely dishy (7, 3, 5)
2 If you take it you won't have so much of it (7)
3 Arranged to be different (5)
4 Paint mixed with poetry on the other side of the world (9)
5 Large-scale water-cooler (7)
6 Feast of the fifties showing all-round growth? (6-3, 6)
7 Inviting in a royal capacity (6)
8 I'm first in grammar! (6)
16 Striking part of one's riding gear (9)
18 Piano fastener in the shrubbery (6)
19 Hold action to be wrong over one point (7)
21 Placed after an attempt in the Games (4, 3)
23 Not happy to have so little time with a girl (6)
25 It's part of the blooming effect! (5)

1
2
3
4
5
6
7
8
9
10
11
12
13
14
15
16
17
18
19
20
21
22
23
24
25
26
27
28
29

5

ACROSS

1 Youngster getting round prohibition in Belgium (7)
5 Come forward with a bill to give up (6)
9 Just a little broth being heated, we hear (7)
10 He can tell us how to alter a Red visa (7)
11 No. 1 in hand (3)
12 The magic of some evening in song (11)
13 Fear there may be an adder around (5)
14 Dropping-in time in Alaska? (9)
16 Resolve to make an end (9)
17 Quick enough for the Navy (5)
19 Screen cry for an actor's appearance? (7-4)
22 Assume a false position? (3)
23 Lack of lively vision in the block (4-3)
24 Understanding of what might be seen within (7)
26 Pour out to remove the humbug? (6)
27 Tale set uncertainly in Washington (7)

DOWN

1 Bird making the vehicle dart around (7)
2 The place for undercover fun? (9, 6)
3 A Roman Catholic Saint's line (3)
4 Something to wear that's different in cut (5)
5 Quite a come-down! (9)
6 The perfumed cat (5)
7 Hopeless engagement landing one in dire trouble? (9, 6)
8 Her wit makes one squirm (6)
12 He was here before the other (5)
14 It may get us into a row (9)
15 Terrible waste, one might almost say! (5)
16 Try to understand the fish in the river (6)
18 Supporter under the table (7)
20 A near miss for a fight venue (5)
21 Something wrong with a spinster (5)
25 Spring back from a state of collapse (3)

6

ACROSS

1 It gives an old fighter a certain distinction (8, 5)
8 The girl I get in the end (4)
9 It goes up in a tree (3)
10 There's a twisted fury about it that's rich! (6)
11 It's instrumental in making Acton nicer, maybe (10)
13 Maltreat in a scrimmage (4)
14 Troublesome products of silver mines (6)
16 Can't beer be made into wine? Yes it can! (8)
19 Not the straight road for Mohammedans to follow (8)
22 Clothing restrictions? (6)
25 It's the same girl coming back! (4)
26 People who get the message look back on the speech (10)
27 The truth in four versions (6)
28 In secret correspondence and so forth (3)
29 As clever as Jack? (4)
30 In which swimmers get their kicks? (8, 5)

DOWN

1 Comfort in the cabinet (7)
2 Just a little, but it's enough (7)
3 Promise of security? (9)
4 Something missing here! (3)
5 Godfather's family? (5)
6 He makes a striking contribution to a noted occasion (7)
7 Of consuming interest in one's salad days (7)
12 Urged to throw tin dice (7)
15 Frenchman's way to regret (3)
17 Flower presented as a fat trophy (9)
18 Short honourable upset in Japanese play (3)
20 Finish the call and break an engagement? (4, 3)
21 It enables one to come clean at the top (7)
23 Postage fiddle by former German officials (7)
24 It may be barred in the garden (7)
26 One wasn't prepared to talk in this way (2, 3)
28 Measure of Kay's following (3)

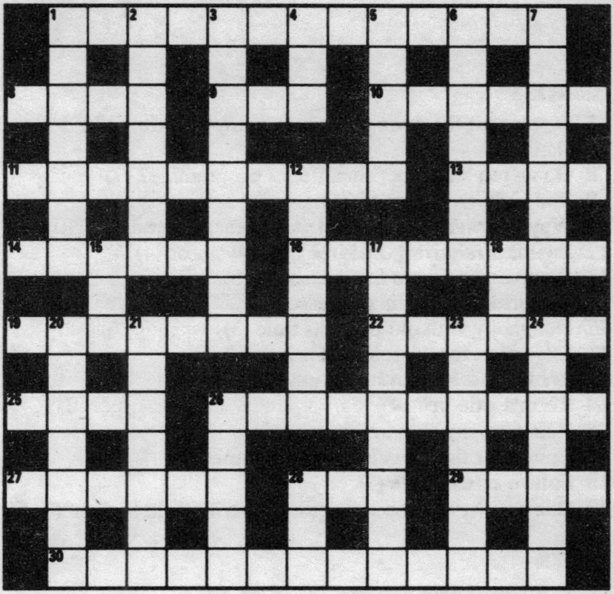

7

ACROSS

1 Getting off the wrong side with many sounding like dogs (12)
8 Go on too long, like an athletics programme? (7)
9 The visitor's vocation? (7)
11 Way the Marines force entry we hear, to see a girl (10)
12 Business requiring a degree of drowsiness (4)
14 Go up and down in the landscape (8)
16 Powerful number in the vessel (6)
17 Not happy with old Bob this time (3)
19 Excursion for the released prisoner? (6)
21 Rebuke a salesman for taking fish (8)
24 Record a tie-up? (4)
25 Half-way sky sign in schools (10)
27 Composer first to get a trophy returned (7)
28 Follow an example (7)
29 One may have to be very quick to strike gold in them (7, 5)

DOWN

1 Saw what might happen (7)
2 Scattering fluid over fifty in one season (10)
3 High points of the Moslem faith (8)
4 Cover for shoppers (6)
5 It enables Mac to show a leg (4)
6 It's disgusting! (7)
7 Emerge the winner of the climbing contest? (4, 3, 2, 3)
10 Allow a city to be given fame by Rupert Brooke? (12)
13 Today's writing (10)
15 For picking up gossip on the side? (3)
18 Contriving ways of leaving to others? (8)
20 CIA plot development in the news (7)
22 Creatures in Alma's orbit (7)
23 Two in one after a sparkling start (6)
26 Doing steady business, no doubt (4)

1
2
3
4
5
6
7
8
9
10
11
12
13
14
15
16
17
18
19
20
21
22
23
24
25
26
27
28
29

8

ACROSS

6 Not the Queen's quality, God save her! (14)
9 Trouble when teacher loses the road (6)
10 Disappeared with kinky Ivan beside a building (8)
11 Stout, stupid group of non-slimmers? (8)
13 Take what you're given! (6)
15 Go down like an acrobat (6)
17 Fabulous creature very confused in some points (6)
19 Tree for bats (6)
20 Virtue of an exclamation (8)
22 Take away in theory (8)
24 Go down with a cry, being uncultivated (6)
26 Triumph of hope over experience Johnson said (6, 8)

DOWN

1 Game of small passes (4, 3, 7)
2 Go up and get the French to look (4)
3 Permits through the mountains? (6)
4 Some darn trouble in docks causing perplexity (8)
5 We have responsibility here (4)
7 Ask to join a party (6)
8 Walking over water one may have their support (8-6)
12 Arrived with a pound for a carrier (5)
14 Do it up to make a lot of money! (5)
16 Depressed areas of Scotland? (8)
18 She might give the chief a different hat (6)
21 They may be acceptable as bargains (6)
23 Weight of antiquity? (4)
25 Year of the quick go-ahead (4)

1 2 3 4 5
6 7 8
9 10
11 12 13 14
15 16 17
18
19 20 21
22 23 24 25
26

9

ACROSS

1 Take the biscuit for a difficult sailing course (4-4)
5 Quick-firing ball of fluff? (6)
9 Frightful raging of the sea for me (8)
10 Enthusiast about the place where there's haddock (6)
12 Make a sound return (4)
13 Cause of a domestic flare-up at school? (5, 5)
15 Down in the valley where there's no work? (9, 4)
19 Opening times (8, 5)
23 The making of a uniform commitment (10)
25 Light indicating special merit? (4)
28 He had his doubts (6)
29 Terry and Ali tied up in writing (8)
30 Provides an alternative to reason? (6)
31 Proceeded on a very uncertain footing (8)

DOWN

1 Gave offence with a blow (6)
2 Get to the limit of personal contact? (5)
3 Try to identify a match (4)
4 Invitation to put a trendy young person in antique furnishing (7)
6 Poppy's stupefying product (5)
7 Makes a point of inducing deflation (9)
8 NCB chief in the West Country? (8)
11 Repeated affirmation of the goddess's existence (4)
14 Time to get across? (4)
15 Dusty lore collected in rambling fashion (9)
16 Help to respond to it (3)
17 Grim party at the old city (4)
18 He won't agree to change the job at first (8)
20 Turn us over to a politician in the depression (4)
21 Sign up in the confusion created by an invader (7)
22 Asked for some divine favours (6)
24 Point to a story that's rather old (5)
26 It may have a following in the countryside (5)
27 Word used for a time in school (4)

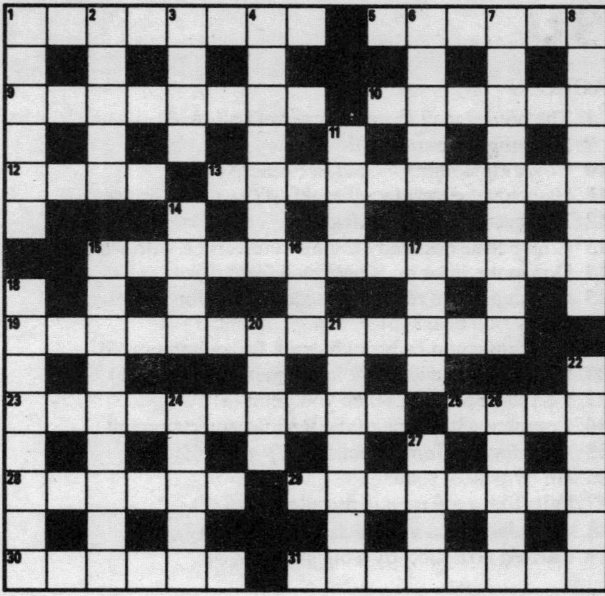
1
2
3
4
5
6
7
8
9
10
11
12
13
14
15
16
17
18
19
20
21
22
23
24
25
26
27
28
29
30
31

10

ACROSS

1 The honest way to meet a cricket ball (8, 3)
9 Standing supporter (7)
10 Covering nothing – and in French! (7)
11 Urge to take the rap at breakfast (3)
12 Tearing about in N. Africa (7)
13 A nice little company roughly concerned with water (7)
14 One in the flock goes back and forth (3)
15 Permit a cry in return for accommodation (5)
17 A boy or a bear? (5)
18 The ship could be brought back for swimmers (5)
20 It should make its mark in the merchant navy (5)
22 Fish to be paid for when you get it (3)
24 Compete with some of the RAF as entertainment (7)
25 Asks for a different decision (7)
26 Hit by way of rebuke (3)
27 Falls like a top man in turbulent Iran (7)
28 Complaining at a protective provision (7)
29 Carried no doubt, by a big shot? (8, 3)

DOWN

1 Oddly enough, it's very peculiar how we can tell (7, 2, 6)
2 Is rough, possibly, but so full of mischief! (7)
3 Bury in ground with no rain (5)
4 Frightful apparition hobbling badly round the ring (9)
5 Only the boldest appear in two underwear items (7)
6 Noting what's said by the man of destiny? (6, 9)
7 Move quickly in past female fashion (6)
8 Troublesome when one wants to get away (6)
16 Great help somehow in giving one the message (9)
18 Rescuing the economy? (6)
19 Not on public display in uniform? (7)
21 Good at causing damage! (7)
23 Plan to provide a new look (6)
25 Stage for domestic drama? (5)

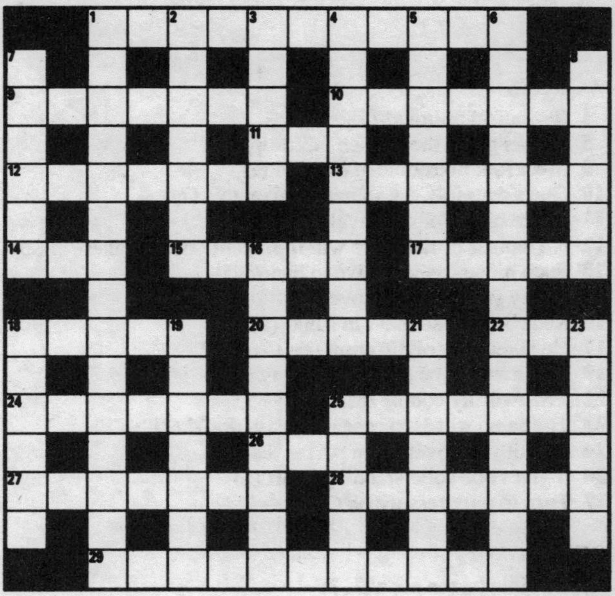
1
2
3
4
5
6
7
8
9
10
11
12
13
14
15
16
17
18
19
20
21
22
23
24
25
26
27
28
29

11

ACROSS

1 Rations of politics? (7)
5 Actors given the French build-up (6)
9 Meet Rex in trouble at one end (7)
10 One's certainly got somewhere on this (7)
11 Strike return of equal value (3)
12 No danger of failing to win if precautions are taken? (6, 5)
13 Such money as you have in hand? (5)
14 Lousy switch ruins move (9)
16 Reds bug me so that I'm sunk! (9)
17 He takes note of different lies (5)
19 You may not be seen in this (11)
22 Trustworthy couple inside (3)
23 The same words to repeat? Please don't! (7)
24 It's got you covered, in part at least (7)
26 It gives one solid standing in art (6)
27 Turn to put pressure on (7)

DOWN

1 Virginia on the prowl? (7)
2 Something to be gained from a gift of cloth? (8, 7)
3 Somebody who might be anybody (3)
4 One's not wanted on this level (5)
5 Hire an accountant? (9)
6 Shoots up to decorate a letter (5)
7 Not the way to reach the Mersey by train (9, 6)
8 Pictures for a cookbook? (6)
12 That's the way to get some of those nasty letters (5)
14 Watch for it! (9)
15 Gold obtained from robbing others (5)
16 Be certain tu look round the dog (6)
18 Possibly not hers to cut down (7)
20 From the performance that's just right (5)
21 People in a row (5)
25 Outfit for a bore? (3)

12

ACROSS

1 Does he use his nails in trying to win? (7, 6)
8 Two-soldier girl (4)
9 It gives one standing in the Information Department (3)
10 More than one is able to identify this bird, it's said (6)
11 Ill-natured person who would walk over the cabbages? (10)
13 Put on weight for profit (4)
14 Stick nowadays at this place (6)
16 At the Boar's Head it's always a long time for a drink (8)
19 One of the coming men (8)
22 Handing out French wine in a carriage (6)
25 Confinement for a hundred at a time (4)
26 Warning to the bank official one can see ahead (10)
27 Put right about a couple (6)
28 It inspired a tale but came back (3)
29 On our side at the end naturally (4)
30 It's laid down for those who are going places (4, 2, 3, 4)

DOWN

1 Inspired by the way Bond didn't like his drink? (7)
2 Rise, change and go to court for a second appearance (7)
3 Not all of the watch? (9)
4 Striking success (3)
5 It's given a lift at the opening (5)
6 Not the first of the brothers (7)
7 Absorbing town? (7)
12 Underground type of steel? (7)
15 Sound active (3)
17 One of those meaty accompaniments (9)
18 A bit of a lift for an Asian, perhaps (3)
20 He doesn't find it a paying game (7)
21 Succeed in putting the clergyman in a vessel (7)
23 Book able to add nothing as a source of hot stuff (7)
24 Made the object of pointed provocation? (7)
26 Do without because of an attempt (5)
28 Little one completely with '29' (3)

1 2 3 4 5 6 7 8 9 10 11 12 13 14 15 16 17 18 19 20 21 22 23 24 25 26 27 28 29 30

13

ACROSS

1 Revolutionary talk, in a manner of speaking? (4, 2, 6)
8 She's repeatedly refused to give a show (7)
9 Equal bargain at the greengrocer's (7)
11 Having one's own way as is common (10)
12 Don't go on returning vessels (4)
14 Going on being faithful (8)
16 He's got it on him (6)
17 One very good at applying a touch (3)
19 Choice of a different point on the ring (6)
21 In which TV gives one the broad view (8)
24 Morning points agreed (4)
25 Going in and putting someone out (10)
27 Hold me back when two appear (7)
28 One can learn from it in perception (7)
29 Does it present a faceless menace? (6, 6)

DOWN

1 Give money a bird in the Abbey (7)
2 Taking back with repeated pulling power (10)
3 How a non-flier can cover the ground (8)
4 Uniform trimming looking pretty hot? (6)
5 Not often Sappers join the Artillery! (4)
6 One star turn in American politics (7)
7 Body of officials who must speak as they find (12)
10 Execution that makes the news brightening the home? (5-7)
13 Cover a diet so that it looks pleasant (10)
15 Man up for some dancing (3)
18 Temporary trouble one may go through (3, 5)
20 Feel a fearful lack of steadiness (7)
22 Isn't Mia around to maintain a soulful theory? (7)
23 Balmy place (6)
26 Barrier to corn in the West (4)

14

ACROSS

6 Altering positions in dressing rooms? (8, 6)
9 Book a top Israelite (6)
10 Philosophical rather than sexual (8)
11 He might not be successful in the long run (8)
13 Being in existence (6)
15 Really giving little information on performance (2, 4)
17 Inherited tendency to stress? (6)
19 Are they worn for brief periods (6)
20 Picturesque cart is it, perhaps? (8)
22 The late school chief doesn't have to pay (4-4)
24 Contrive to upset the new gal (6)
26 Permanent instructions as to status? (8, 6)

DOWN

1 Something attempted, something done (14)
2 Where it all comes out (4)
3 Horrified at the misshapen hags inside (6)
4 Seeming a quiet father or mother (8)
5 A month on circuit in Ireland (4)
7 Neck linen? (6)
8 Philosopher for the time being? (14)
12 Conclude as a consequence (5)
14 Catches one's luggage (5)
16 Comes round with a small movement to improve looks (8)
18 Pet all-rounder? (6)
21 Getting on to where the patients are (6)
23 Finished being swindled? (4)
25 One's very inadequately supplied in it (4)

15

ACROSS

1 Not much room for a singer, perhaps (4-4)
5 Coster in confinement (6)
9 Time for fun to be provided by Ivan and Carl (8)
10 Take it easy, Walker . . . (6)
12 . . . and take it easy as a sitter! (4)
13 Publicity rating for an old bed? (4-4)
15 Not favouring talk of a denial (13)
19 No overnight declarations in this (3-3, 7)
23 Overtax resources to improve his turn (10)
25 Move in a most irksome way (4)
28 Five hundred and ten in cold absurdity (6)
29 Ragman about to be given a bill for brandy (6)
30 Times when one puts letters in order (6)
31 Proceeded to lend money? (8)

DOWN

1 Bend to fasten (6)
2 Right range in the country (5)
3 Cut out at speed (4)
4 Olga tiddly with run has some attraction (7)
6 Perform better in the open air? (5)
7 Possible choices for a job of no great stature? (5, 4)
8 Rent a lot, maybe, without being too particular (8)
11 Frame for current distribution (4)
14 She comes up just the same (4)
15 Economical aspect of the City (9)
16 Tune for radio? (3)
17 Taken for a top performance at teatime? (4)
18 Parrot noises being the art of government, we hear (8)
20 It would be wrong for the horse to follow it (4)
21 Having paid for protection (7)
22 Adorned by a princess? (6)
24 Having something to say about the song (5)
26 Note it does one good? (5)
27 No. 1 place for a miracle (4)

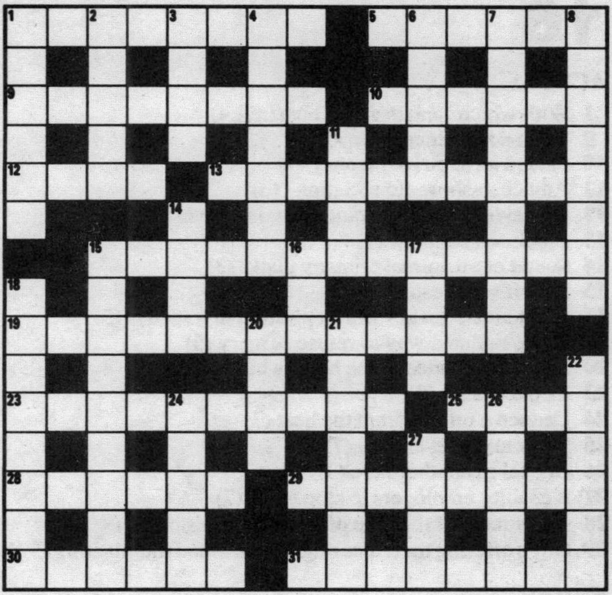
1 2 3 4 5 6 7 8 9 10 11 12 13 14 15 16 17 18 19 20 21 22 23 24 25 26 27 28 29 30 31

16

ACROSS

1 With which Jack ties up a boat? (7, 4)
9 Train a former reporter (7)
10 Said to have put out money (7)
11 Advice to show appreciation? (3)
12 Go beyond when not quite certain to overtake (7)
13 Blocks on the floor (7)
14 Sound of an animal or many ducks (3)
15 Put off with respect (5)
17 Light music-maker with aspiration in tragedy ((5)
18 Probe to find a way to refuse surgery (5)
20 Something added to the horse's burden (5)
22 It covers a pit (3)
24 Deduce a refusal from the heat (7)
25 Show nude pet around (7)
26 One takes another here (3)
27 It enables employers to stop work (7)
28 Adornment of the time of Victoria, possibly (7)
29 Guy's offering that Nero might have found illuminating (5, 6)

DOWN

1 One's out-ranked by him in service (8, 7)
2 Trawlermen could experience some coolness here (7)
3 Removes from encounters Jay didn't get to (5)
4 Kay left the upper decks in a wreck and was sunk (9)
5 As you'd expect, not a flat! (7)
6 No change required for travelling in it (7, 8)
7 Send Uncle by air what's thrown overboard (6)
8 Rioted around as a journalist (6)
16 What's-his-name may be such a man (9)
18 Falls at the lights? (6)
19 Act according to procedure (7)
21 Make a comeback in new covers? (7)
23 Many speak in low tones (6)
25 Nutty product of a police artist (5)

1
2
3
4
5
6
7
8
9
10
11
12
13
14
15
16
17
18
19
20
21
22
23
24
25
26
27
28
29

17

ACROSS

1 Turns down whistle-blowing jobs (7)
5 The act of a twister (6)
9 She may want to know what's in store (7)
10 One of the three allowed to follow the outing (7)
11 Service a long way back (3)
12 No great force to prevent one reaching the heights? (3, 8)
13 The doctor chap is a fool! (5)
14 Chairman's removal is required by this philosophy (9)
16 Having the possiblity of power (9)
17 Stately way to knock back a beer (5)
19 Turn Lily on to Mae, with feeling (11)
22 Knowing where to draw the line, maybe? (3)
23 In which one feels one's getting somewhere (7)
24 Fuel vessel? (7)
26 Be there before midnight and start dancing (6)
27 Lent car for circulation in the inner area (7)

DOWN

1 It gives the speaker higher standing (7)
2 All the way through (4, 5, 2, 4)
3 Drink a little for half the meal (3)
4 Hat you might see on a farm (5)
5 Drop in the river (9)
6 Gives out at different times (5)
7 It makes a difference to the look of processed food (9, 6)
8 Movement from the Gulf (6)
12 Material for a railway point (5)
14 Made to feel strange when a date-line is wrong (9)
15 It may be the thing to do after paying cash (5)
16 Good-looking? Rather! (6)
18 Mistake not to use imagination (7)
20 Dispute in the paper (5)
21 Colour of a shrub (5)
25 Smith knows how to make one (3)

18

ACROSS

1 Behave badly towards someone you think is a clod? (5, 4, 4)
8 Paddy's produce (4)
9 Same material dropping a point (3)
10 Enclosure of key meaning (6)
11 Yielding to pressure in quiet speech? (4-6)
13 Every single one (4)
14 Waist that's divine in the distance (6)
16 Dense crowd providing the stout (8)
19 Apes Jean deviously as an Oriental (8)
22 Very good bill-head marvellous! (6)
25 They're not long for the favourite (4)
26 Limited as to speed in such an area (10)
27 Attacked for being drunk? (6)
28 Somewhere to drink in Plato country (3)
29 Extent of the square, apparently (4)
30 Mad determination to be king? (6, 7)

DOWN

1 Journey to distribute oil in North Africa (7)
2 Crossed by most supporters (7)
3 Bit of beastly extension? (9)
4 Annoy some of the long-hair kids (3)
5 She has the measure of the quarters (5)
6 Threatened by a possible future mate (2, 5)
7 It may flow sweet and slow (7)
12 Youngsters given equipment numbers (7)
15 Go down quickly for a light (3)
17 Writes as a donor (9)
18 Watch the thing boiling (3)
20 Ones called to account by him (7)
21 The team for powerful shooting (7)
23 Confession of wrongdoing by Vic Cape (7)
24 School where things are done differently (7)
26 Bit of a row and a lot of noise made by a sculptor (5)
28 Signal irritation? (3)

19

ACROSS

1 Where they always try to improve the instruction? (6, 6)
8 A French policeman may get Irma in trouble (7)
9 Money for repast I sent round (7)
11 They're taken from unwilling payers (10)
12 Backroom Othello (4)
14 Here's someone new (8)
16 Uniform making one look unhealthy? (6)
17 Responsibility for a hit (3)
19 It may be moved to give new directions (6)
21 A fan as it might be in music (8)
24 Support a return (4)
25 Patient endurance of a rotten oil change (10)
27 Not inclined to make contacts (7)
28 Englishman of the East (7)
29 The time a harp moved to accommodate an audience (12)

DOWN

1 Have fun with one in the list (7)
2 He's quick enough to get there ahead of the others, it seems (10)
3 Item by item he disposed of stock (8)
4 Lying back to see us up a tree (6)
5 Take in some of the arts (4)
6 Result of the extrusion process (7)
7 Mama's blue ire can be very great (12)
10 It tells of an attack before it happens (5, 7)
13 Perplexed one good man in an air current (10)
15 This service makes the fish look flashy (3)
18 He's no ruddy Indian! (4-4)
20 Recite a refusal to demand money? (7)
22 It could be the death of one (7)
23 Harm an animal on the way (6)
26 Desire for some sort of bone (4)

20

ACROSS

6 Continue to take appropriate steps! (2, 4, 3, 5)
9 A girl needs a chap some days (6)
10 Person of degree (8)
11 Nobody asked him! (8)
13 Cut out that tax (6)
15 Disreputable-looking fun person? (6)
17 Put away what the good fellow should have paid (6)
19 Look at the old boy back in the pavilion! (6)
20 Welsh travel service preventing one going overboard? (8)
22 I perform subsequently as an admirer (8)
24 Leave when you might extend service (6)
26 Being sold in battered condition? (5, 3, 6)

DOWN

1 By no means rare at Clapham or Kew? (6, 2, 6)
2 Move around like a bird (4)
3 Seashore yarn (6)
4 Waterfront container? (3-5)
5 Get on for something to eat (4)
7 Heraldic cover derived from bad art (6)
8 Handy sign that one hopes for the best (7, 7)
12 Go up in the French way, you rascal! (5)
14 Shrink into a business we get right at last (5)
16 Defector from a river country (8)
18 Fail as a consumer (6)
21 Loud over moral ruin without departing from decorum (6)
23 Right to take the wrong line (4)
25 A certain number seem this way to me (4)

21

ACROSS

1 Accessory carrier alternative to sleeping-bag? (8)
5 Plant a drink on a pet (6)
9 Told off to have the end removed (8)
10 Old chap at the end of the line? (9)
12 Atmosphere in which a girl loses her head (4)
13 Bound to appear in false teeth? (10)
15 Take-off sketches? (5, 8)
19 Go to extremes to keep fit (5, 4, 4)
23 I vex the USA in a way that could be tiresome (10)
25 Something to wear in error (4)
28 Unable to take the long view (6)
29 Apt not to be on the level (8)
30 Retain movement in the eye (6)
31 Suggestions are acceptable in this state (8)

DOWN

1 Take away a child having a sleep (6)
2 Make a later amendment (5)
3 Cut for a bargain (4)
4 Make a lot of money as a char? (5, 2)
6 No longer a minor figure (5)
7 Villainous four in sea change (9)
8 He's like another writer, funnily enough (8)
11 Not quite top-rate in Greek (4)
14 Bridge may be held up by it (4)
15 One way to get a drink in Merseyside (9)
16 It may be given to the next speaker (3)
17 Removed to give approval (4)
18 Ribbon in the wind (8)
20 Financial jotting? (4)
21 Quite a number even in poor accommodation (7)
22 Suit some diggers? (6)
24 We're at one in this (5)
26 School punishment taking certain directions (5)
27 Scheme to expose the layout (4)

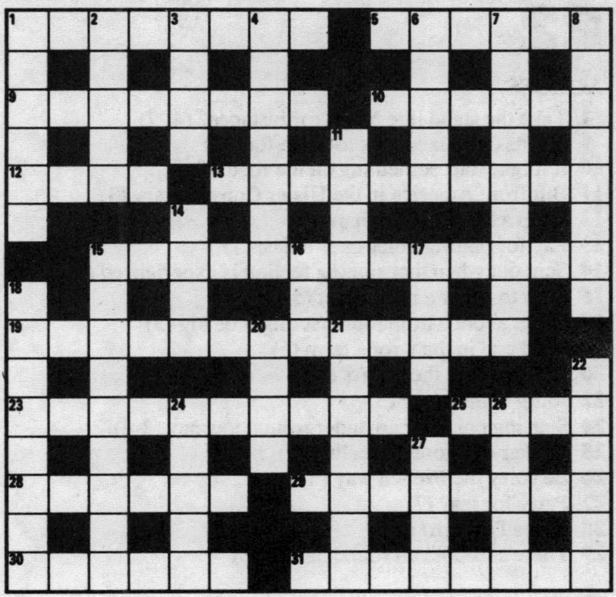

22

ACROSS

1 Take the stand like Yogi, for instance? (4, 7)
9 Hands out mixed gins to some fool (7)
10 It might start something on the road (7)
11 Bill from America in the Ulster Constabulary (3)
12 Keep a bit of fish in shape (7)
13 Pay for putting holes back at last (7)
14 Sent out when that sinking feeling is experienced (3)
15 Start to cheer a river beast (5)
17 Shout about a little foot that might be big (5)
18 Send one in the wrong term (5)
20 Campaign in the papers (5)
22 Jump in the beer? (3)
24 Starting point for an underground journey (3-4)
25 Stinker of a foreign feeling (7)
26 Be sorry the French way (3)
27 Party for tea? (7)
28 States I'm a girl (7)
29 There's trouble all round here (5-6)

DOWN

1 They're used to get things done in company (8, 7)
2 Breaking out in a gush to express suffering (7)
3 We sat around not wanted (5)
4 Solid reminder of a departure (9)
5 The sort of talk we understand (7)
6 Where the cops-and-robbers film shows the action? (5, 2, 3, 5)
7 Shows one is moved by the music? (6)
8 Lofty as the proverbial drink (6)
16 Vision of leading the Highland Regiment? (4-5)
18 Fame is the ruin of upperclass Peter (6)
19 Lot more shaky in play (7)
21 Having the answer to the problem of dissolution? (7)
23 Have a shot at a chap in the pub (6)
25 Not one of those Roses of the War (5)

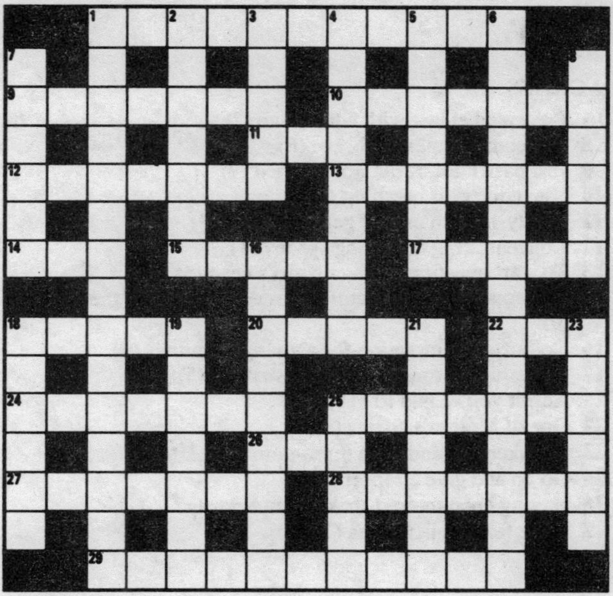

23

ACROSS

1 Presented at last with what's due (7)
5 It accommodates the brave (6)
9 Just hasn't got it, but not worried (7)
10 His industry is catching (7)
11 A fifty-fifty chance of getting the lot (3)
12 Concentrating on saving space (11)
13 To start questioning over a girl's head (5)
14 Someone needing treatment for eccentricity in the engine? (9)
16 Colourless temptation for a young swimmer (9)
17 Something wrong with a non-striker? (5)
19 Admit you've had it! (11)
22 One of Mother's sisters (3)
23 It's taken in hand for a three-point attack (7)
24 Go up and give a report (7)
26 Having encountered striking superiority? (6)
27 Little fellows in the sea (7)

DOWN

1 Lent age in order to look smart (7)
2 For dancing at a run? (6-5, 4)
3 Deceiver's tangle? (3)
4 Vision of five hundred on paper (5)
5 Source of a cleansing shower on the move (5-4)
6 Inform about the hashish? (5)
7 Possible fill-in for a vacant post (11, 4)
8 Accent on the shoe (6)
12 Possible changing-point for a company on the way (5)
14 Dishonest cleaner with a South African set-up (9)
15 Jack in hand (5)
16 Plenty of money is common in Australia (6)
18 They may gain ingress as entertainers (7)
20 Not hiding the ring on the green (5)
21 Do it up for a special occasion (5)
25 Knock up a perfect score (3)

1 2 3 4 5 6 7 8 9 10 11 12 13 14 15 16 17 18 19 20 21 22 23 24 25 26 27

24

ACROSS

1 Striking reciprocity among insurers (5, 3, 5)
8 Turn to become an old European (4)
9 Ice cream in the bath (3)
10 Going out to make a seashore exposure (6)
11 Girls in the locality almost striking? (4-6)
13 Substantial volume as far as I'm concerned (4)
14 Grounds for contesting titles (6)
16 Snuggling like a young bird (8)
19 Rush mats deep in trouble (8)
22 One might get in to gain it (6)
25 Put up an elevation (4)
26 Being recognised by the heralds is, perhaps, our Reg's aim (10)
27 Fighting doctor in a jacket (6)
28 Favourite (3)
29 Claim the clothing back (4)
30 Just a whiff of the common Market? (6, 7)

DOWN

1 Most eager to see Kent in a new way (7)
2 Regulated by decree (7)
3 Bird to rouse the cat? (9)
4 Little brother coming up for a ball (3)
5 They're up for a Cockney dance (5)
6 Going round to take part in exam (7)
7 Relative from an island? (7)
12 Warm smile in the light? (7)
15 First man not to finish as a girl (3)
17 Pole finding amusement that's simply killing (9)
18 Cold petrol engine (3)
20 Peter out without an end? (4, 3)
21 Beast that swallowed the label may be changed (7)
23 Animal with a bone in the middle (7)
24 Wise about the states of food (7)
26 Act it out in a room (5)
28 Weasel noise (3)

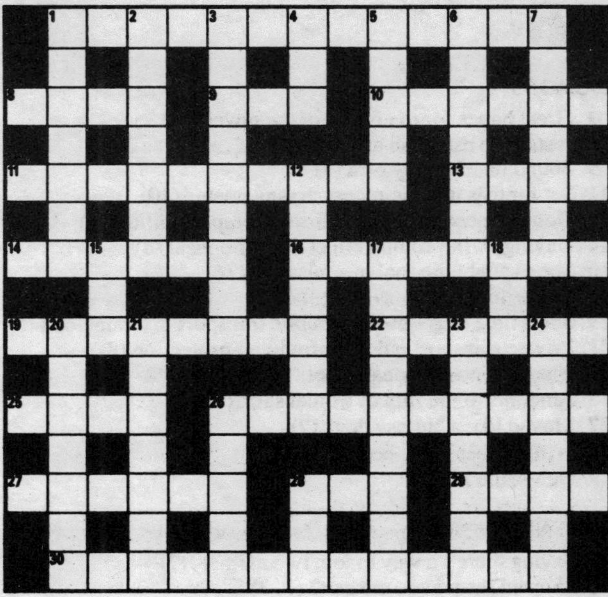
1
2
3
4
5
6
7
8
9
10
11
12
13
14
15
16
17
18
19
20
21
22
23
24
25
26
27
28
29
30

25

ACROSS

1 Great hopes for the future of the novel (12)
8 It starts to establish an identity (7)
9 Sound like a happy bird (7)
11 Set for teas in anticipatory arrangements (10)
12 Douglas needs it with his foreign responsibilites (4)
14 Having an improving effect on a dire meal (8)
16 She's caught the fool in a falsehood (6)
17 The wife's brother's in it! (3)
19 Short time to get back by public transport in a raincloud (6)
21 Private transport quickly providing protection (8)
24 Island in international waters (4)
25 Amounts to the ruin of a quiet saint (10)
27 Moved like a clumsy dog? (7)
28 Win another place here (7)
29 He's made it! (12)

DOWN

1 Saying there's a way to join two animals (7)
2 Showed the way to the exit? (7, 3)
3 Very big deficit in fuel (8)
4 Old fighter in a radio family (6)
5 I take a bit of a risk for her (4)
6 Afraid to finish dinner with you Frenchmen (7)
7 It is not always the same gear? (12)
10 They were here before us (12)
13 The soldier's manoeuvre might put beer in a car (10)
15 Bill under fifty and yet in the red (3)
18 Cart a Northerner around the wall (8)
20 Goddess appearing to wrench an arm vein (7)
22 Man of high endeavours (7)
23 It's plain frozen! (6)
26 You singularly old-fashioned person! (4)

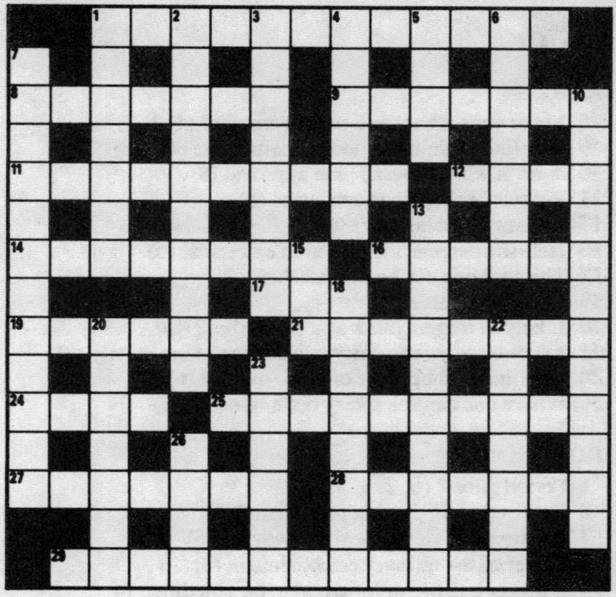
1
2
3
4
5
6
7
8
9
10
11
12
13
14
15
16
17
18
19
20
21
22
23
24
25
26
27
28
29

26

ACROSS

6 Make quite a haul as a puppet-master? (4, 3, 7)
9 Gentleman about to mock a formidable lady (6)
10 A form which doesn't gain approval (8)
11 Vessels broken up in sea terms (8)
13 Reason for being low? (6)
15 Hellish characters if turned to extremes! (6)
17 The cool one can be hot stuff! (6)
19 Light contrasts (6)
20 Likely to make a mark as a bad writer? (8)
22 Accountant briefly party to a change of air in Italy (8)
24 Gets the push because of a pub quarrel (6)
26 Where one can see a very hot angle (4-4, 6)

DOWN

1 Period ghost? (6, 2, 3, 3)
2 Get tired of displaying patriotism? (4)
3 Position Di takes to be some way off (6)
4 Power of the military establishment (8)
5 It makes it difficult for wood to be sent direct (4)
7 Pass another way please (6)
8 The pious folk next door? (4, 10)
12 I'm the last to change (5)
14 Small hooter (5)
16 Dirt as it might appear to the absent minded (8)
18 It might be made in an unexpected departure (6)
21 Subject of a colourful tie-up (6)
23 Friend following form in matters of ceremony (4)
25 Like a bell when stepped on? (4)

27

ACROSS

1 One of those present at a Scottish gathering (8)
5 Old fool at a party with Jack at the Duke's Head (6)
9 Determined to make Rose hop to a musical instrument (8)
10 Foreign fighter just an illusion? (6)
12 Liberate for nothing (4)
13 They may be part of a very hot build-up (10)
15 Sentiment of the household? (6, 7)
19 More than enough to remove a red pub suntan (13)
23 Showing colours going down at last (10)
25 Keep the cash here – and how! (4)
28 Has tag amended in horror (6)
29 That heel could be a killer ! (8)
30 Irritating on purpose (6)
31 Forceful connection in superior style (5, 3)

DOWN

1 Bottle artist in refreshing surroundings (6)
2 The way to the altar (5)
3 Old man of the sea (4)
4 Scene of the workers' rising (3-4)
6 All-round rise arranged for basket-makers (5)
7 Ian's chart may show him not to be law abiding (9)
8 Wise to follow Reds around in an equestrian event (8)
11 Complain about the meat (4)
14 Nothing to spoil a poet (4)
15 Affected in a way (9)
16 Second person to take part in the Sunday outing (3)
17 Brief inquiry to what you know (4)
18 He hopes for higher things (8)
20 Support from behind (4)
21 Always going on about perpetual motion? (3-4)
22 News of an explosion (6)
24 Sense of derangement in Germany (5)
26 High up in the ancient Greek world? (5)
27 Sorry about Peter being about to depart (4)

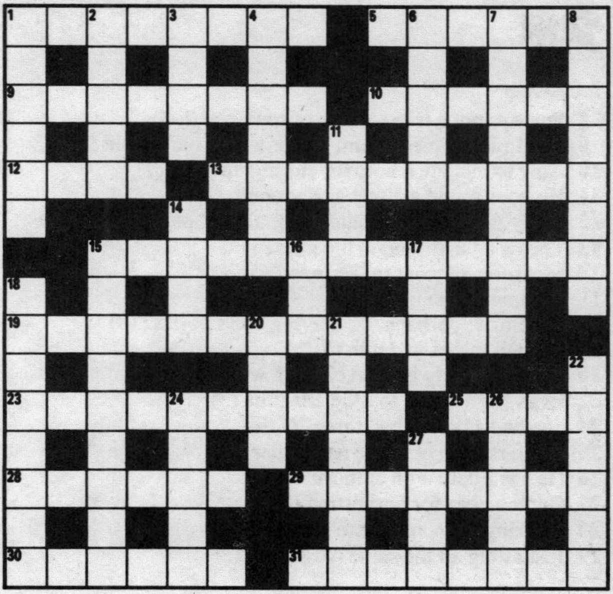
1
2
3
4
5
6
7
8
9
10
11
12
13
14
15
16
17
18
19
20
21
22
23
24
25
26
27
28
29
30
31

28

ACROSS

1 Perhaps not a true retailer of romance (5-6)
9 The low creature in him :nakes a man unreliable (7)
10 Able to include a note for cutting up meat (7)
11 He goes round a circle at Plymouth (3)
12 Study the kind that could make a royal partner (7)
13 Throw a lie around in the garden (7)
14 Measures of print in Germany (3)
15 A name for nobility (5)
17 Eccentric, perhaps, but having one's points? (5)
18 Go into things in depth (5)
20 He might stray around chasing women (5)
22 Eggs are nothing to little Virginia (3)
24 She had a box of bad things (7)
25 Set in motion at a cute new order (7)
26 He has a date with authority (3)
27 Get together for harvesting (7)
28 Looking for someone to shoot (7)
29 Just as big all the same (4, 3, 4)

DOWN

1 He doesn't talk about his muscles (6, 6, 3)
2 Mail dispatch branch? (7)
3 Man of distinction in a rising river craft (5)
4 Very good at getting out of prison? (9)
5 It's not easy to get a rise out of him! (3-4)
6 They move in political circles, of course (15)
7 There might be a saving if one comes to it (6)
8 Slippery as Grey might be (6)
16 Will wayward mates be in temporary accommodation? (9)
18 Show a PC tied in knots (6)
19 Feeling the Number One Book raises (7)
21 The following train (7)
23 Make retribution for Geneva's destruction (6)
25 Try to get a bite at the corner (5)

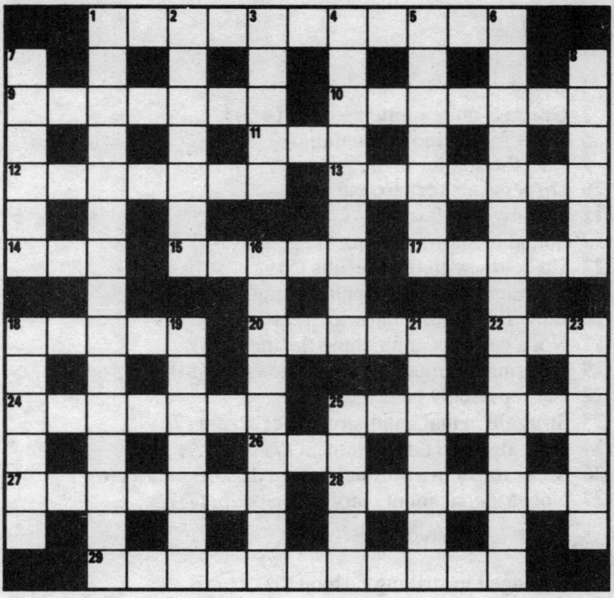

29

ACROSS

1 One gets quite immersed in it (4-3)
5 Don't forget about phoning! (6)
9 Like the soldier in the Abbey (7)
10 Disperse art sect around (7)
11 Go downhill fast (3)
12 Sound of approval from the gods? (7-4)
13 Go below with fatal results (5)
14 Harmless enough though starting in a pub (9)
16 Lure Ted in for a midway pause (9)
17 Not a bad shot at finishing the meal! (5)
19 Offering too much on what one's told (11)
22 Cat repeatedly beaten (3)
23 Struggle in that confusion to get across (7)
24 Like nights of entertainment (7)
26 Mean to get in a number before darkness starts (6)
27 Note a signal about recording a poem (7)

DOWN

1 Damaged in striking fashion (7)
2 Accept a blow relating to a personal point (4, 2, 2, 3, 4)
3 One's follower (3)
4 African turning the nut to some degree (5)
5 One lives in some style here (9)
6 Taking it may involve loss of standing (5)
7 Half a loaf? No bread? The alternatives don't offer much! (6, 2, 7)
8 Tries to make contact in the dark (6)
12 Course for a singer? (5)
14 Flooded in without the day being noted (9)
15 Don't let go of that peach! (5)
16 The pressure's the same all along the line (6)
18 A tale of two churches (7)
20 Not afraid to be at home in America (5)
21 This is something like! (5)
25 Said to be everything that's boring (3)

1
2
3
4
5
6
7
8
9
10
11
12
13
14
15
16
17
18
19
20
21
22
23
24
25
26
27

30

ACROSS

1 Something valuable that's been dug up (8, 5)
8 Said to be in for a lot (4)
9 Dawn riser (8)
10 Move in and get the General Staff to arrange departures (6)
11 Knowing enough to talk about it? (10)
13 Basis of a drink offer (4)
14 Can see trouble when messages come from the other side (6)
16 Understood to have made the grade another way (8)
19 It's nothing for me to allow Ted to start making a dish (8)
22 They're made to be taken up (6)
25 Man causing a hold-up (4)
26 There's still opposition when the rent case is amended (10)
27 Hide or display (6)
28 Form a link in patience (3)
29 Continue to be an absurd character (4)
30 Where that dear old lady came from? (6, 7)

DOWN

1 Aim to turn up with different prose (7)
2 Excite the archdeacon after a change of line (7)
3 Rebellious person under the broken ruins (9)
4 Holder of the ashes (3)
5 Strength of a possibility? (5)
6 Plant that might get you down (7)
7 The stuff we drag around with us (7)
12 Rags lie around in Africa (7)
15 Lincoln familiarity (3)
17 A collection for the bride (9)
18 Not straight whisky we hear (3)
20 Mum, Doc and I in a little confusion (7)
21 Hit the crooked with a light touch (7)
23 A little French will get anything filled (7)
24 Sink a politician, say, at Church House (7)
26 Grazing land in mountains? (5)
28 It's just a little moving (3)

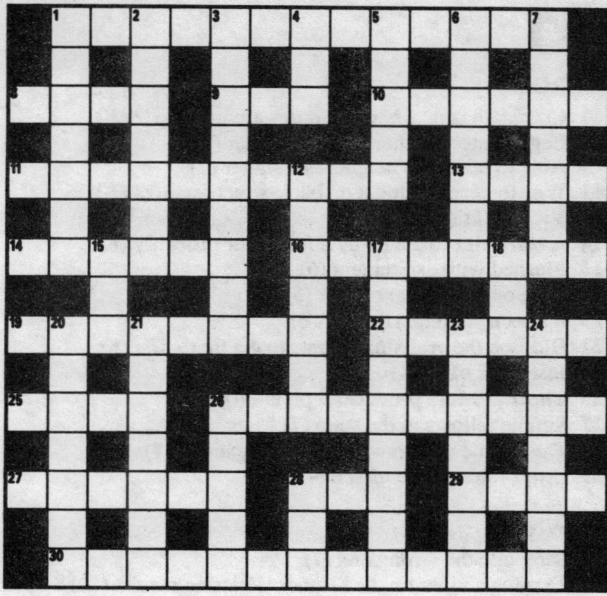

31

ACROSS

1 Complain is it, when meanings are involved? (12)
8 Beg to enter another way at the rear (7)
9 Able to reach the heights as a singer (7)
11 Way to get agreement on back-street features (10)
12 Victim of the fall (4)
14 A bad hull broken up by a foreigner probably (8)
16 Flushed with excitement (6)
17 Note on Anglo-Saxon talk (3)
19 It's been stretched this far (6)
21 Old Bob the craftsman wants to get there first (8)
24 Just think of it! (4)
25 Cheer as Mum produces a pipe! (10)
27 Simple fellows in the soup (7)
28 They come and go with unfriendly intent (7)
29 Old soldier on the march (7, 5)

DOWN

1 Sang into the wrong end (7)
2 Turning a viper on the heather is getting results (10)
3 Got it! But the claim may be made in advance (2, 3, 3)
4 They may be possessed in groups (6)
5 I join a little chap among the Zulus (4)
6 Sea tern going round to the most convenient point (7)
7 Indication revealing an informer? (4-4, 4)
10 Chaps in charge don't seem to have got things sorted out here (8, 4)
13 Most charming old hag in existence (10)
15 Obliged to be in possession (3)
18 Extra support for the pork eater? (5-3)
20 It sounds as if one's shaky as a musician (7)
22 Decorative detective work? (7)
23 One way is set up for a girl (6)
26 Such a voice could get her completely (4)

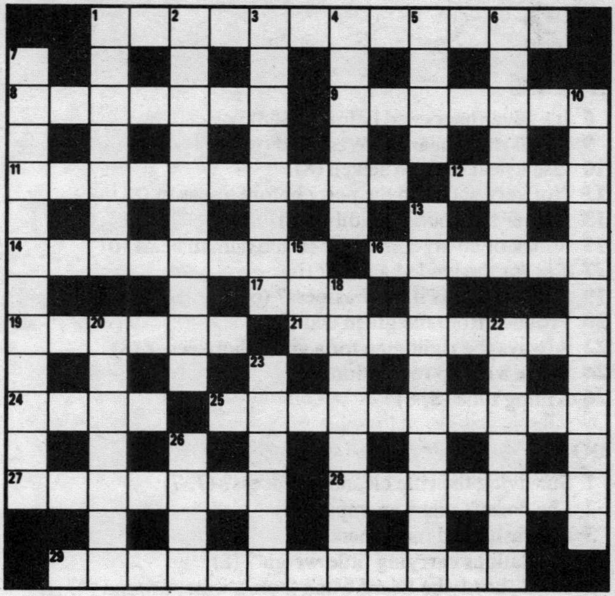
1
2
3
4
5
6
7
8
9
10
11
12
13
14
15
16
17
18
19
20
21
22
23
24
25
26
27
28
29

32

ACROSS

6 It's never happened before! (6, 8)
9 Small room near the West End (6)
10 Use a neat twist to sicken (8)
11 Not very active in the party before a season (8)
13 Scatter the young untidily? (6)
15 Shock of an art comeback on the human heart (6)
17 Car for the landed gentry? (6)
19 Suffering or is it just business? (6)
20 Produce from the green end (8)
22 Always the right man for a good shopkeeper (8)
24 Brave a cheap revolution (6)
26 Killing time (8, 6)

DOWN

1 Surviving the rifle cleaning process? (7, 7)
2 She doesn't make an impact (4)
3 Old fashioned movement? (6)
4 Hesitations carrying little weight? (8)
5 I will shortly be heard when there's water around (4)
7 One art in which the decoration is overdone (6)
8 Calling from a distance (2, 3, 9)
12 Talk of nothing but local payment (5)
14 Bridal transport? (5)
16 The cowman's girl? (8)
18 Pull again at something infuriating (3, 3)
21 Serious learner starting on the drive, perhaps (6)
23 Means of bringing up the plunder (4)
25 Spring up with a point in church (4)

33

ACROSS

1 Preface with what might be said to be a warning (8)
5 Fighting to get a doctor into a jacket (6)
9 Lying supporter (8)
10 Beat with a kindly touch (6)
12 There's just one thing (4)
13 Wooden whiskers? (10)
15 Picture a show-girl helping to prepare woodwork (5, 8)
19 Doing an all-round political turn (13)
23 There'll be none of this if people aren't let in (10)
25 Where to start looking for a Siamese (4)
28 Kindly get out of Ealing! (6)
29 Chap who's mature having various qualities (8)
30 It could be used to remove a deposit (6)
31 Something more to tack on finally? (8)

DOWN

1 Car fib may be material (6)
2 Crest a bird might part with (5)
3 At their end is distraction (4)
4 Fighting Muhammad in repose has no illusions (7)
6 Act better in the Open Air Theatre? (5)
7 Life in the library (9)
8 Try a ruse to get into office (8)
11 Known in the South-East? (4)
14 He may put forward a paying proposition (4)
15 They're trodden underfoot in the city (9)
16 Among the riskier ways to make a quick descent (3)
17 One front could be Russian (4)
18 Organised a break from the grand era (8)
20 It's very hard to get a meal at the King's Head (4)
21 There should be plenty of pickings here! (7)
22 Hurried to get a Benedictine when out of control (6)
24 The business of the winds (5)
26 Southern promise of fighting (5)
27 Road away from the fighting that's prevalent (4)

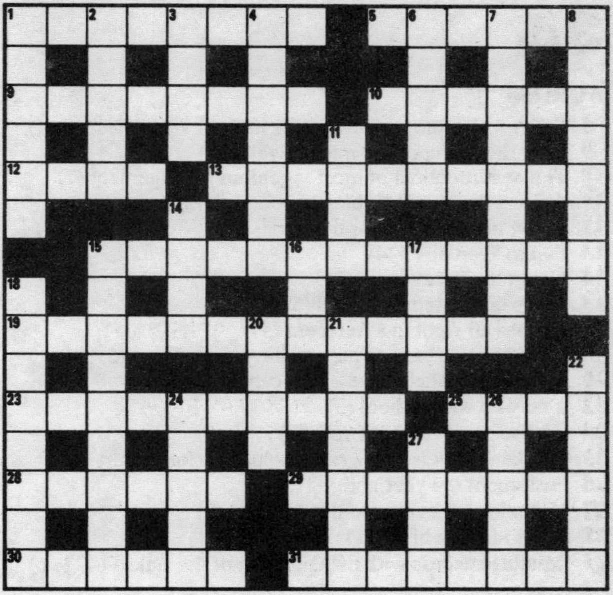
1
2
3
4
5
6
7
8
9
10
11
12
13
14
15
16
17
18
19
20
21
22
23
24
25
26
27
28
29
30
31

34

ACROSS

1 From which the restaurant fills its staff vacancies? (7, 4)
9 Only the unimportant might rival it (7)
10 Ten-seat runabout of most ingenious arrangement (7)
11 Among the chief troubles of pond life (3)
12 A dog may be right for the miner (7)
13 Fail to keep up (3, 4)
14 It's set for the evening (3)
15 Temp taking temperatures (5)
17 Frames all right in agreement (5)
18 Bring the fish back to me and have some wine (5)
20 Point in the lake where a man can be seen (5)
22 It may be wise to hoot (3)
24 Hit back and cut at the root (7)
25 Chicken provided by a railway lubrication expert (7)
26 Fuss about the year nothing (3)
27 Met rain – that altered the garment (7)
28 Make idle use of thumbs (7)
29 Possible success with fifty per cent of the stake? (4, 1, 6)

DOWN

1 Foreign devotee of spin (8, 7)
2 A letter of personal introduction (7)
3 Having less to do than a lounger (5)
4 They're not rough with ladies (9)
5 Tiny pal in unsuitable fashion (7)
6 Growing understanding in the Garden of Eden? (4, 2, 9)
7 Old punishment for investors? (6)
8 They're rolling in a group (6)
16 Pale actor miscast in Shakespearean role (9)
18 They don't seem happy about some PR arrangement (6)
19 Hide on occasion inside (7)
21 Mine, too, many somehow express feeling (7)
23 There is usually food in store for us here (6)
25 Make a bad job of it (5)

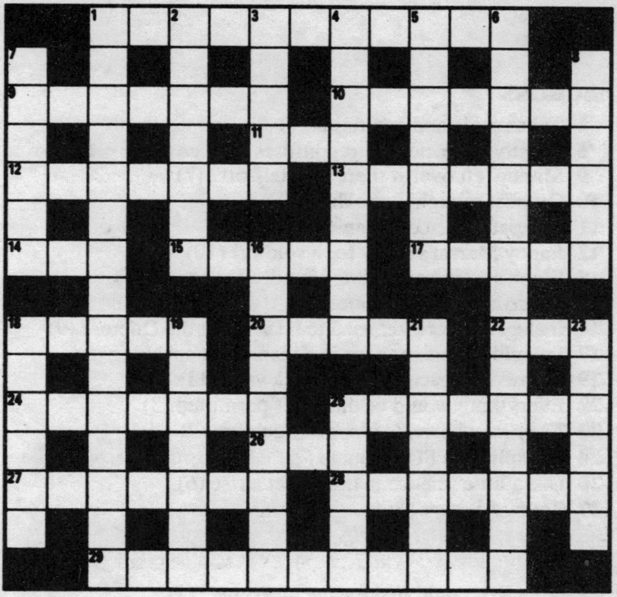
1
2
3
4
5
6
7
8
9
10
11
12
13
14
15
16
17
18
19
20
21
22
23
24
25
26
27
28
29

35

ACROSS

1 Takes aside and entertains (7)
5 Beastly characters Bert confuses with us (6)
9 Money left over if there's no fall-off? (7)
10 Oil pact brought up to date (7)
11 Sympathetic accompaniment (3)
12 Fanny Martin's crazy for a soldier! (10)
13 Flook's friend appealing soundly for cover? (5)
14 Set up a technical school (9)
16 Inelegant as cricket used to be without the Doctor? (9)
17 I would get one honour in a manner of speaking (5)
19 Dismiss a structure in the back yard (11)
22 Everything would be on tick if permitted (3)
23 They may be made if sport is corrupt (7)
24 Big split if in SOS trouble (7)
26 Use a little science at last to get a rise (6)
27 Love of a story (7)

DOWN

1 Bet a Red could make quite an arguer! (7)
2 Such common pieces have no place in the decimal world (6, 9)
3 The way to get off the airfield (3)
4 Quieten a little chap on the ledge (5)
5 Flora may fascinate them (9)
6 Such a cut could have a striking impact (5)
7 Church outing in a sense (15)
8 Look strikingly oblique (6)
12 Send out a number (5)
14 Idle aside regarded as perfect (9)
15 Cake covering flight danger (5)
16 Grown-ups lose points in sets (6)
18 She gives me a line that isn't straight (7)
20 Lets's get together to do it (5)
21 Deduce from a finer realignment (5)
25 One may do it up in case (3)

1 2 3 4 5 6 7 8 9 10 11 12 13 14 15 16 17 18 19 20 21 22 23 24 25 26 27

36

ACROSS

1 Turning on a feeble ruse that couldn't be known beforehand (13)
8 Couch reduced for a singer (4)
9 Plant at a dance? (3)
10 One must rise to attain it (6)
11 He holds a position of corresponding importance (10)
13 Curves lightly between terminals? (4)
14 Feels painfully well turned out? (6)
16 Depend on taking money in not long ago (8)
19 Drive away from the hunter's house (8)
22 News of the French trial (6)
25 Agitation in the kitchen (4)
26 Notorious expert taking one in spoken form (10)
27 Does he take a bow as a radio character? (6)
28 Description of some sailor's sin? (3)
29 There must be a way of escape from it (4)
30 Centres on a place in Cumbria and Cleveland (13)

DOWN

1 Dress alike (7)
2 More even than praise? (7)
3 Put in some practice before play started (9)
4 Try to acquire a taste (3)
5 The air there is different (5)
6 In this country we keep it in mind (7)
7 Can it be moral to hit Alec badly? (7)
12 Tube traveller (7)
15 Did the Vicar of Bray sound like one? (3)
17 Name the last person in Scotland? (9)
18 Do it up at the end of a boat trip (3)
20 One might confuse the miner with it between events (7)
21 Made staggering progress (7)
23 Picture at a blue roundabout (7)
24 Laborious point at which to be generous (7)
26 Danger from a spirit over half a century (5)
28 It may be an opportunity if it's missed (3)

37

ACROSS

1 Just what the doctor ordered! (12)
8 Comprehensive cover (7)
9 Devour a bird? (7)
11 Trains do it in time-honoured ways (10)
12 Heated outcome when a top is blown (4)
14 Upset about a music-hall act (8)
16 Hard for a clergyman coming back into a diocese (6)
17 Try to finish the idle talk (3)
19 Press man at the top (6)
21 The player hasn't eaten everything (4, 4)
24 Former morning test (4)
25 Dishonest rule at fund conversion (10)
27 The tick may be lost in the shrubbery (7)
28 Mix-up in a male game that lacks finality (7)
29 There are fifty in America (6, 6)

DOWN

1 A few words before the confrontation? (7)
2 Result of having a thin time (10)
3 Men of the underground sometimes at sea (8)
4 There's no sense in Annie's new look (6)
5 One might join it for kicks (4)
6 Cattle-food served at a Texas tea-party? (3-4)
7 It's all rather off-putting (12)
10 Great occasion for a big swimmer? (5, 2, 1, 4)
13 Tear about the street air finding somewhere to eat (1)
15 Nothing but an endless line-up (3)
18 Cross girl leading the Bible section (8)
20 Foreigner raising a point after one expression of gratitude (7)
22 Vindicates even gas possibly (7)
23 Worn away with irritation? (6)
26 The way equipment can be made a mockery (4)

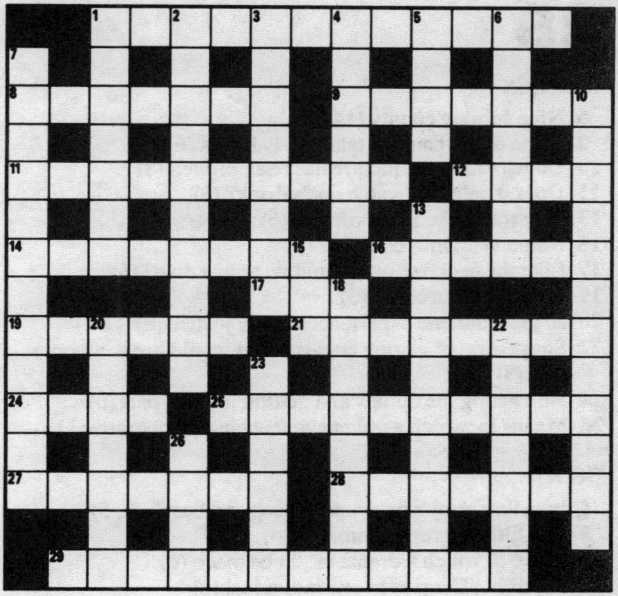
1
2
3
4
5
6
7
8
9
10
11
12
13
14
15
16
17
18
19
20
21
22
23
24
25
26
27
28
29

38

ACROSS

6 Nine furlong county (14)
9 Some of the banquet taken in Pakistan (6)
10 Quite certain the picture has been printed (8)
11 Does it help one watch one's drink? (8)
13 Any rot can be made official (6)
15 Name William's conquest (6)
17 Like the neckline one would wear in a dive? (6)
19 It must have a cause (6)
20 In the wind one experiences faulty justice (8)
22 Suggestion of getting engaged that would break up poor pals (8)
24 He's acting the outlaw and getting into the part (6)
26 Means by which a union avoids being co-operative (14)

DOWN

1 Invading army's pressure to keep one busy? (9, 5)
2 The filth that turns stomachs (4)
3 Force of which a drama might be made (6)
4 Possibly offensive to one individual (8)
5 It could be put in a sporting event (4)
7 Remove from a sitting? (6)
8 Echoes even to barriers, perhaps (14)
12 Eat too much Cheddar? (5)
14 Course for a singer (5)
16 Such a temperament a painter may have! (8)
18 A beast given tea, say, might display charm (6)
21 It enables one to change sides in a depression (6)
23 There could be a tie-up here (4)
25 Deal pointedly with a lie? (4)

1
2
3
4
5
6
7
8
9
10
11
12
13
14
15
16
17
18
19
20
21
22
23
24
25
26

39

ACROSS

1 Unfortunate lack of resilience? (4, 4)
5 It has its points as a plant (6)
9 Only one stray oil move (8)
10 Pure although pursued, it's said (6)
12 Something missing here (4)
13 Depending on a group of soldiers (10)
15 Instrument showing the strength of a demanding body (8, 5)
19 Rules broken in taking border people to a back street (13)
23 Waves the horses' feed containers (10)
25 She is herself either way (4)
28 Going out all round (6)
29 Share of the earnings, or the other way round (8)
30 She may be hidden in cupboard or cask (6)
31 Break for a young bird (3-5)

DOWN

1 Put on pressure to get a move on (6)
2 Reminder of Eric's confusion about a pound (5)
3 Not in time for survival (4)
4 Odd how nosey one can be! (7)
6 Very pale, like a Light Sussex? (5)
7 Do they give the eater a growing sensation? (5-4)
8 Put away in case (8)
11 Performer of various arts (4)
14 Half the points on the motorway (4)
15 Poisonous creature to publicise a calculating machine? (4-5)
16 Work in a large house (3)
17 The group can get along in Scotland (4)
18 Many old houses are half this (8)
20 Blow the end of the month! (4)
21 We'll have to get together for it (7)
22 Such wood as may be underfoot (6)
24 It would be a help if she turned up (5)
26 She's relatively pleasant about an early start (5)
27 Get together for an X performance (4)

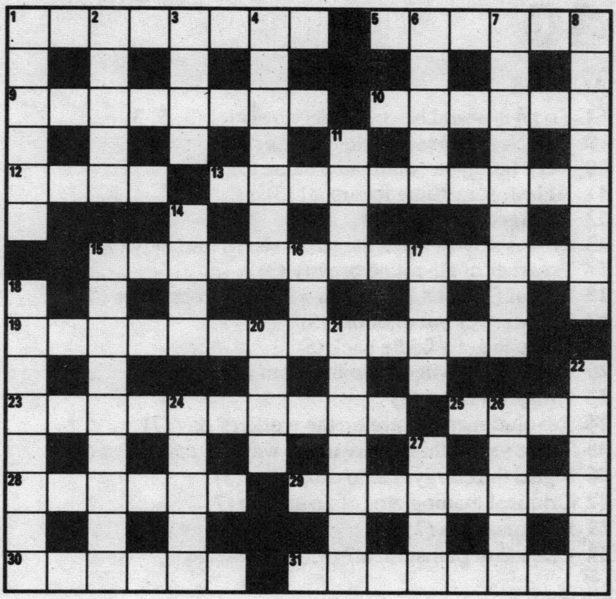
1
2
3
4
5
6
7
8
9
10
11
12
13
14
15
16
17
18
19
20
21
22
23
24
25
26
27
28
29
30
31

40

ACROSS

1 To go it would be completely beastly! (3, 5, 3)
9 Ask Nora to provide the jackets (7)
10 Very little you could put a name to? (7)
11 At last, something to aim at! (3)
12 Enlarged at length (7)
13 Moves slowly when the street seems unsteady (7)
14 Preacher of all-round brevity (3)
15 One of Caesar's killers has a fall and loses notes (5)
17 Takes cover out of doors (5)
18 Game to get a fiddle back (5)
20 Concerning what's missing from a perm (5)
22 Crazy fastener! (3)
24 Revolutionary centre on the workers' day (7)
25 There's something fishy in the way she concludes (7)
26 Signal the clergyman to drop a rat (3)
27 Criminal manipulator of an art trio (7)
28 Beat musician (7)
29 Climate of punishment? (4, 7)

DOWN

1 Having fifty per cent. excess brain-power? (3, 6, 2, 4)
2 Can be longer in Castile (7)
3 Washed with one's socks on? (5)
4 Goes ashore at a point where one can get a picture (9)
5 Epic of domestic riches when he's gone (7)
6 Cultivated cultivator? (9, 6)
7 Look, it's a bird! (6)
8 Demands an end to those bottles (6)
16 Does it cause a fearful deviation from straight flight? (9)
18 I'm tidy, swathed about in cotton (6)
19 Cut down what may be not hers (7)
21 Finished being penetrating ? (7)
23 Of them, was Henry the Eighth? (6)
25 The ways news gets out (5)

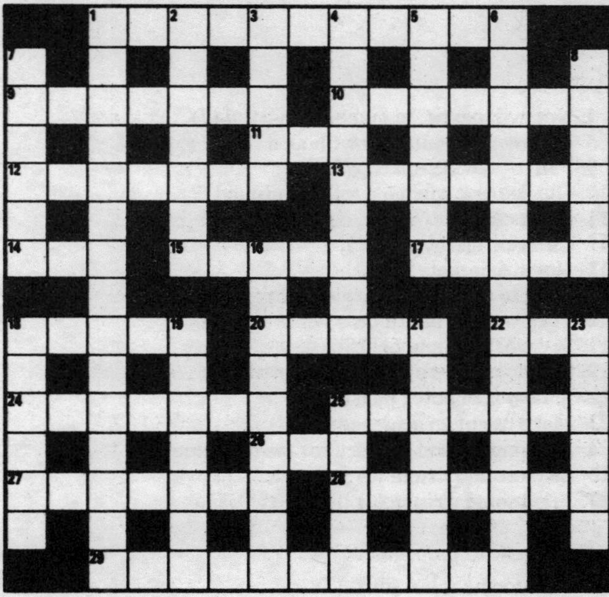

41

ACROSS

1 Not evil maybe, but possibly hurtful (7)
5 Bloomer or youngster without a pound (6)
9 Fail to provide upkeep (3, 4)
10 Quick drink when the ref isn't around (7)
11 Great character who's lost colour (3)
12 Carry on clergyman! (5, 2, 4)
13 Not this or that (5)
14 Release a builder to be a member of society (9)
16 They weren't here a little while ago (9)
17 Say what it might be! (5)
19 One doesn't give him free hospitality (6, 5)
22 In favour of being paid (3)
23 Make use of an achievement (7)
24 A raging around in space for the first time (7)
26 Be there and listen! (6)
27 Tried some writing (7)

DOWN

1 Its outcome is hot stuff! (7)
2 Where one won't get hit in passing (3-2-3-3, 4)
3 For instance, there's nothing here but oneself (3)
4 Bucking up with the gin? (5)
5 They can see they may have something to say (9)
6 Bluff fellow? (5)
7 He stands to gain from the transaction he's involved in (10, 5)
8 Pencil a note on the cloth (6)
12 Leo's follower among the stars (5)
14 Loaded a number when Fred came round (9)
15 Expressing a powerful possibility? (5)
16 Head sleeper? (6)
18 Like a woman in a hell of a fury? (7)
20 Nothing in front for the fatal coil (5)
21 Imperial flier (5)
25 Fuel, in the main (3)

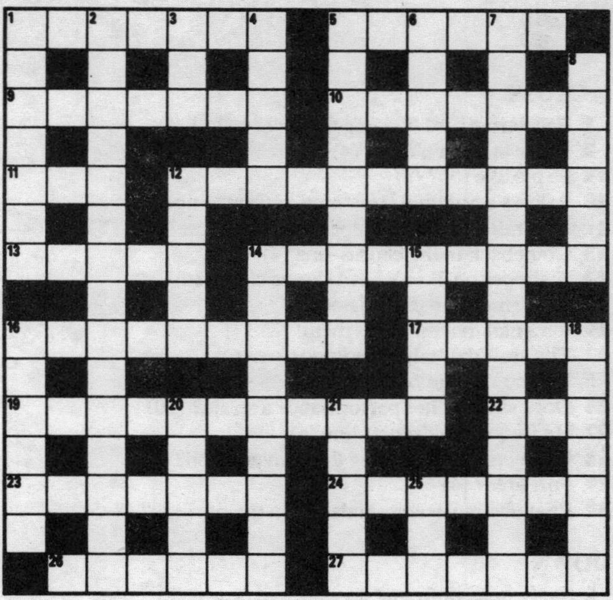
1
2
3
4
5
6
7
8
9
10
11
12
13
14
15
16
17
18
19
20
21
22
23
24
25
26
27

42

ACROSS

1 Pedestrian bird heading the set? (4, 2, 3, 4)
8 Ruler in certain cases (4)
9 Explosive top? (3)
10 Allows a nominal streaming in Cambridge (6)
11 Neutralise the shopkeeper's performance? (10)
13 Comeback in the chorus-line (4)
14 A slipper on Tom's head shows charm (6)
16 Enduring change not later (8)
19 It's a nail that unsettles them! (8)
22 The stuff that might be important (6)
25 Put the knife in Saint Jack (4)
26 Does she find her performance a strain? (10)
27 He frequently drops a line (6)
28 Little creature catching the conversation? (3)
29 Port area? (4)
30 Reallocating accommodation in the pavilion? (8, 5)

DOWN

1 Study behaviour and do what's expected (7)
2 Means of communication with France? (7)
3 Players in sound combination (9)
4 Suggestion of a reward? (3)
5 Said to have consumed a number (5)
6 Lover of unprofitable play (7)
7 Know about irritation in the home (7)
12 Star Ian as a worker (7)
15 States from various angles (3)
17 Such dull sweetness? (4-5)
18 Ready to fit (3)
20 Big enough to have sunk (7)
21 Oil able to be used for plant conversion (7)
23 Rent over a party storm (7)
24 Makes certain of not starting rebukes (7)
26 Make a show of irresponsibility (5)
28 He's big at Westminster (3)

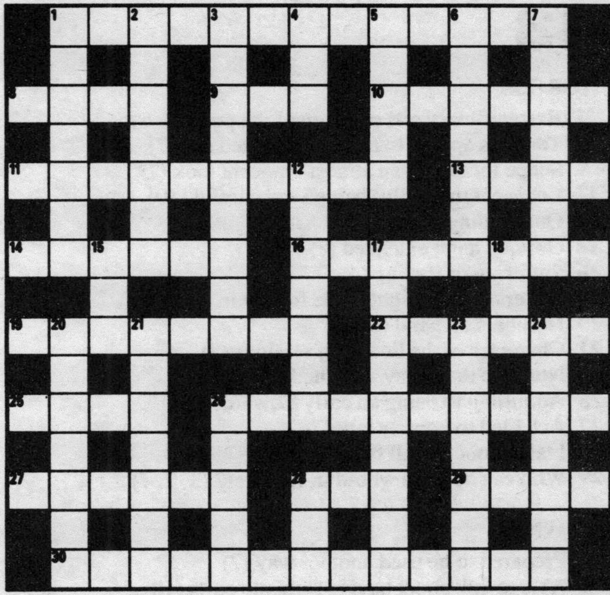

43

ACROSS

1 Extraordinary girl once top of the pops (7, 5)
8 Tar does appear to have been hotted up! (7)
9 Scope for taking an almost innocent look (7)
11 Louis cut me badly, being very careful (10)
12 Outstanding cover? (4)
14 Oblique flank extended (8)
16 Suffering or trading (6)
17 Water or beer might come from it in turn (3)
19 Numbers on hand (6)
21 Character of the licensing sessions (8)
24 Not here to display a method (4)
25 Admitting to being an early Edward? (10)
27 Act 1 led to homely talk (7)
28 I talk about myself being one (7)
29 Who can he be, a who-dun-it writer? (3, 2, 7)

DOWN

1 Prepared to be used another way (7)
2 Able to talk about having separate parts (10)
3 Not doing much to disentangle net on lid (8)
4 Mineral cheats them its said (6)
5 Excellent! It's not often one can say that! (4)
6 Conditions in which mail, etc., is diverted (7)
7 Pledged an estate in Israel? (8, 4)
10 Their craftsmanship facilitated earlier revolutions (12)
13 The White House wasn't built of it (5, 5)
15 Gift of a lot of talk (3)
18 Tenders publicity bids (8)
20 Trouble and a rag in Spain (7)
22 Three in college (7)
23 Low comedy character (6)
26 One can't agree to use it (4)

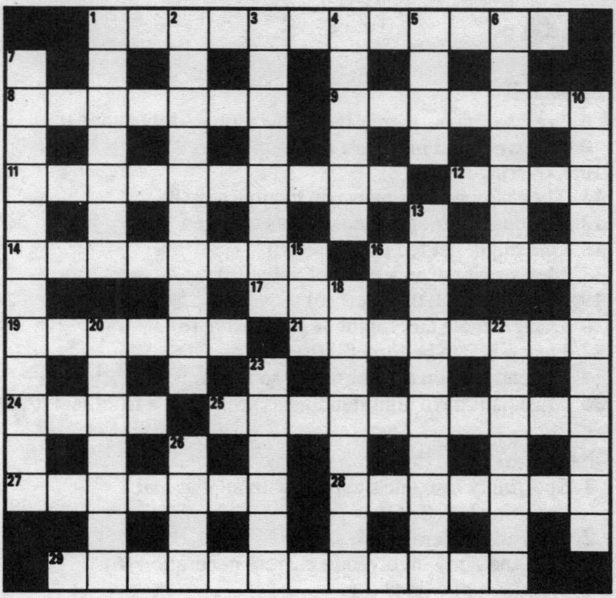
1
2
3
4
5
6
7
8
9
10
11
12
13
14
15
16
17
18
19
20
21
22
23
24
25
26
27
28
29

44

ACROSS

6 Wait a minute, there's the ostler's job to do! (4, 4, 6)
9 Girl we found in Nora's make-up (6)
10 Covering letter! (8)
11 They may give us pause on the journey (8)
13 The character of the tea urn has changed (6)
15 One might get fed up with it (6)
17 Meets reverse on a point of value (6)
19 Have a bash at the beer! (6)
20 Disagreeable talk might be persuasive (8)
22 I teach MP to be forceful (8)
24 Expenditure on a going-away song (6)
26 Musicians have high standing as seen from a front seat (9, 5)

DOWN

1 Sportingly lose one's temper with all that nail knocking? (5, 3, 6)
2 Cold and miserable (4)
3 Don and Amy involved in current generation (6)
4 Whiskers of wood? (8)
5 Examination of the mouth (4)
7 Difficult when assurance is lacking? (6)
8 In a trying way (14)
12 When you add it up – what have you got? (5)
14 The gas you pay for (5)
16 It's relatively helpful to a well-connected youngster (8)
18 She gives a moving performance (6)
21 Bird with a complaint? (6)
23 A laugh in the depression (2-2)
25 Transport organised on urban lines (4)

1 2 3 4 5
6 7 8
9 10
11 12 13 14
15 16 17
18
19 20 21
22 23 24 25
26

45

ACROSS

1 Twice knightly performance (8)
5 Road up or just lethargy? (6)
9 New Foreign Office arrangement predicted (8)
10 No rags could make such an attractive garment! (6)
12 Order a straight line (4)
13 Bloomers for motor races (10)
15 Where there's scope for climbing (8, 5)
19 All round it's the same distance from the centre (13)
23 Linked as it's a code (10)
25 Fine stone of the Episcopalian Church (4)
28 Old bird in hot water (6)
29 A number of changes of tint in landing (8)
30 Not liable for a former temp's aberrations (6)
31 As far a beauty can sink in? (4, 4)

DOWN

1 Give what you can pay for (6)
2 She'll get a hearing at Christmas (5)
3 Promising accompaniment for sketchy ablutions (4)
4 Talk at length about harmony? (7)
6 Characteristic of it to follow Cleopatra's end (5)
7 Say the word! (9)
8 Put your name down, just for the record (8)
11 Not in favour of some of this gallivanting! (4)
14 Singer getting a couple of lucky starts (4)
15 Stamps up and down like clockwork? (5, 4)
16 No. 1 peformer in a race (3)
17 It shows how far one's come up in the Service (4)
18 Hurry to get an egg for breakfast? (8)
20 Something wrong with one's standing, it's said (4)
21 Eggs a dashing fellow to identify an animal (7)
22 Respond sportingly to provoke rage? (4, 2)
24 Unpleasantly quiet character? (5)
26 In sitting one has to show a certain dignity (5)
27 Soon to be seen in a negative direction (4)

1 2 3 4 5 6 7 8
9 10
11
12 13
14
15 16 17
18
19 20 21
22
23 24 25 26
27
28 29
30 31

46

ACROSS

1 New get-up for players of old (6, 5)
9 Continuing on departure (7)
10 Panicky female? (7)
11 Some household purpose (3)
12 Small look at what's published officially? (7)
13 No longer working in bed (7)
14 Go after this dance (3)
15 The cider drinker's companion (5)
17 Noise showing it won't work? (5)
18 It may have to be faced bravely (5)
20 More remote when the route is altered (5)
22 Cut-price cube (3)
24 Cancel a request to make a speech (7)
25 Helps by being present (7)
26 Creature sounding hoarse in a circle (3)
27 Easily seen to plunge back with the wrong net (7)
28 Vases won at the shooting gallery? (7)
29 It's said to be childishly rued (7, 4)

DOWN

1 Bit of newspaper in which some powder's kept? (8, 7)
2 Rudderless craft? (7)
3 Police gallery man? (5)
4 Putting off may neutralise the agitation (9)
5 Took just what was right? (7)
6 More than sound progress (10, 5)
7 Acquired hog but went astray (6)
8 Game for a crossing (6)
16 Boring game leading up to an explosion? (4-5)
18 More disturbed by one of the reds (6)
19 Was it built for the defence of French wine? (7)
21 Food provision might turn to riots (7)
23 Tries to put into words in a letter (6)
25 Put on to be demanding (5)

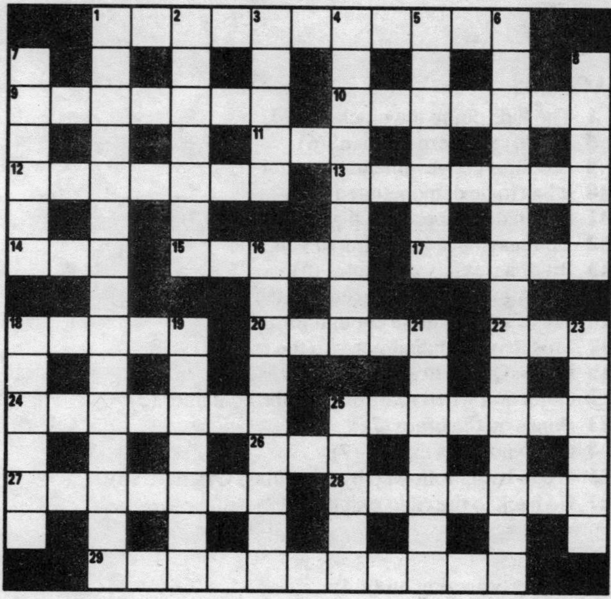
1
2
3
4
5
6
7
8
9
10
11
12
13
14
15
16
17
18
19
20
21
22
23
24
25
26
27
28
29

47

ACROSS

1 The kids doing the pinching? (7)
5 Talk of a Liverpool man! (6)
9 A coin is convertible into capital (7)
10 It has to be demonstrated (7)
11 Indian or Chinese often getting drunk (3)
12 You may have it coming to you (11)
13 Bit of a mix-up with notes (5)
14 Way of making the queen itch (9)
16 There's never quite enough for this (9)
17 Most trivial amendments to the tales (5)
19 Like a Queen in style (11)
22 Objection when returning for the container (3)
23 Bones on the brain (7)
24 One who has a calling (7)
26 We're being followed by a headless Oriental! (6)
27 Go back to the right exit (7)

DOWN

1 Always carrying on (3-4)
2 Breaks from work in the parcel department? (7, 8)
3 Letters to a German resort (3)
4 Destroy with a big hit (5)
5 Rail Act is, perhaps, just being funny (9)
6 Not hidden on the tree-top (5)
7 Players of four-line composition? (6, 9)
8 Don't help when I'm deep in trouble (6)
12 Clumsy write-up in it (5)
14 He out-manoeuvres the smart dean in business (9)
15 It's the very fibre of any Londoner's being! (5)
16 Parts of it are the grammar book (6)
18 Heraldic covers (7)
20 Wonders awaited her underground (5)
21 Fly without getting anywhere (5)
25 Decline to turn up the heater (3)

1
2
3
4
5
6
7
8
9
10
11
12
13
14
15
16
17
18
19
20
21
22
23
24
25
26
27

48

ACROSS

1 Medium for after-dark art? (8, 5)
8 Declare the short road to be right (4)
9 On paper it enables one to make one's mark (3)
10 Don't like being despatched again! (6)
11 So excited about lack of inflation? (10)
13 His lordship is nearly in New York! (4)
14 Take off the outside end and convert to a workroom (6)
16 How one may sit with advantage? (8)
19 Talk right round? (8)
22 Makes an impression in craft work (6)
25 Take the top position in a most arbitrary way (4)
26 They may be sought by those in doubt (10)
27 Sum given for a horse (6)
28 Write with an enclosure? (3)
29 Support a retreat? (4)
30 Show noted for jokes? (7, 6)

DOWN

1 Always allowed round to see the little beast (7)
2 She's in the swim at last! (7)
3 Familiar figure with a hood in the district (9)
4 A number comes here to get the scent (3)
5 Where to get plastered? (5)
6 Look quietly into a small creature's heart (7)
7 Shoot a climber (7)
12 Be quick to say it! (7)
15 Turn to the Navy for a vessel (3)
17 Spare Eton from misuse of language (9)
18 The man at the Russian end (3)
20 It's best to choose one parent (7)
21 Powers of being good? (7)
23 Unworthy to make one glib amendment (7)
24 Cloying in a sticky way (7)
26 A race to be in charge at the top (5)
28 No card at the big house, mate! (3)

49

ACROSS

1 Where you play, how you decide who starts – that's the whole game (5, 3, 4)
8 A lot may be knocked down in it (7)
9 Danger of a mystical incantation not loud enough (7)
11 I find Tom is in deep trouble, in short (10)
12 Half of life with Mother is capital (4)
14 Arty Czech? (8)
16 Wasting no time in sour gentilities (6)
17 Mean not to try to be a friend (3)
19 Famous for interrupting the bowling (6)
21 You can bet it's a card game! (8)
24 Club used for the hard strokes? (4)
25 At length it produces music in Australia (10)
27 Brave man with the ladies (7)
28 One thing one might read in the paper (7)
29 Bird of rough spirit, one hears (6, 6)

DOWN

1 Full of mischief sporting on the ice? (7)
2 Contrived by a man to cover a woman (6-4)
3 Does it cause difficulties in Lincolnshire? (8)
4 You can get it by telephone (6)
5 Cover a number and start again (4)
6 Starting play in church? (7)
7 Encounter a strikingly superior opponent (4, 1, 7)
10 He's in business professionally (12)
13 Law agent paid to manage a museum? (10)
15 Catch up with prohibition (3)
18 All that talk could be bad, curse it! (8)
20 Made visible after dark (7)
22 He wants a lot of change in politics (7)
23 Gain Rugby points in such cold weather! (6)
26 Musical covering? (4)

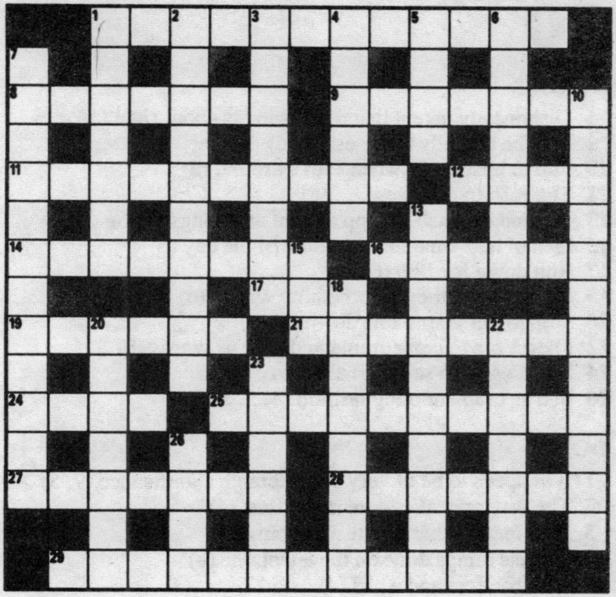
1
2
3
4
5
6
7
8
9
10
11
12
13
14
15
16
17
18
19
20
21
22
23
24
25
26
27
28
29

50

ACROSS

6 Dishonestly take it that a thousand is about right (14)
9 Kill the old lady in the estate (6)
10 Fun to upset Ivan when Carl's around (8)
11 The rush to get away . . . (8)
13 . . . and the rush to drop a point as a songster (6)
15 Idea of half-time in the middle of the day (6)
17 Run down for Bob (6)
19 Desert when there's something wrong (6)
20 Stop to put your name down (8)
22 I beg Vera to come round and give us words (8)
24 Have a go at a sailing manoeuvre (6)
26 In true crap-shooting fashion (8, 2, 1, 3)

DOWN

1 It happens to be of very considerable significance (9, 5)
2 The way one takes note in the East (4)
3 Bath feature that's quite absorbing (6)
4 He gets things done on the telephone (8)
5 Two soliders and a girl (4)
7 Old and new force in transport (6)
8 They're easily seen through (14)
12 On your head be it, Bishop! (5)
14 They may be repeated all the way (5)
16 Go further away to the mountains (8)
18 Stop, perhaps, to become a starer (6)
21 Such a look as one might expect from an artificial eye? (6)
23 Constabulary rhythm (4)
25 Not the sort of sum you get in tattered notes? (4)

51

ACROSS

1 Elevated entertainment drink (8)
5 Steals some bad beer (6)
9 Attempt to get round Pat's follower with a note of deception (8)
10 Having been taken to Len's possibly (6)
12 Flat girl on a pole (4)
13 Kills amusement on board (10)
15 Where one might make library reservations? (7-6)
19 Ignore the stock where the prices are cheaper? (8, 5)
23 Product of a high level of cultivation (4-6)
25 Determination to make a late distribution (4)
28 Likely to get the push from an unestablished retailer (6)
29 In which one is outvoted (8)
30 Too much to be paid for perhaps (6)
31 Veteran of the Victorian era? (3-5)

DOWN

1 Knock the girl about this way! (6)
2 Appearance of bonfire characters, it's said (5)
3 Prepare thirteen to the dozen? (4)
4 Rock singer! (7)
6 Fascinating old woman (5)
7 Crush super-evil into dust (9)
8 Left looking evil (8)
11 Hurry to take note of a foothold (4)
14 The no-partner game (4)
15 Pibroch is given variations in ecclesiastical office (9)
16 Crazy twister (3)
17 An animal rises in the stream (4)
18 It's lovely to be capable of getting round a girl (8)
20 Informer hurried up at the start of the killing (4)
21 No ordinary copper (7)
22 He may provide notes for our enjoyment (6)
24 Big enough to square a dozen (5)
26 South of France rising about nothing, so to speak (5)
27 Run away with some material (4)

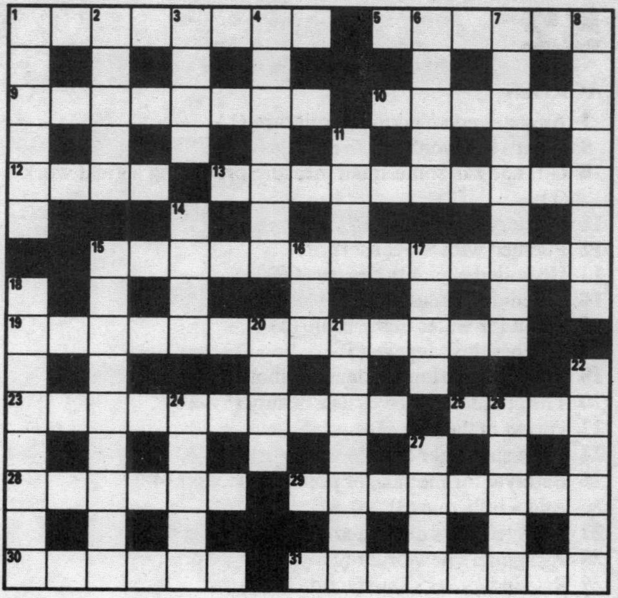
1 2 3 4 5 6 7 8
9 10 11
12 13 14
15 16 17
18 19 20 21 22
23 24 25 26 27
28 29
30 31

52

ACROSS

1 Anger at poem taking a fruit turn (11)
9 What's left won't fall over (7)
10 Girl and I in some small measure producing a great work (7)
11 Mystery river? (3)
12 Pursued with a cleanser? (7)
13 He boiled at eighty degrees (7)
14 Scheduled as suitable (3)
15 Shout for water in the Bible (5)
17 Catches the baggage (5)
18 Record occasion for dancers shortly (5)
20 The archdeacon gives us a beauty (5)
22 Period in the rain (3)
24 Bible supporter (7)
25 Betrayal for the sake of popular success? (4-3)
26 Add a little one (3)
27 Set free Jack's demented love (7)
28 A ragman's new order (7)
29 Rise in worker's satisfaction (3, 8)

DOWN

1 Do better not to expose the ankles? (4, 4, 5, 2)
2 My French supporter is king! (7)
3 Wanting too much of a note on the wood-wind (5)
4 Find out where a nice star has gone wrong (9)
5 Hard man taking on a worker (7)
6 Derby is over here (5, 10)
7 Reviled for possibly finding us a bed (6)
8 Notches up at least forty points? (6)
16 Interviewed about what happened at an early age (9)
18 Girl calling up an artist for money (6)
19 Cover with too many eggs? (7)
21 Fruity female at an Eastern court (7)
23 Changing hats with the old lady causes disorder (6)
25 The case of the domestic flight (5)

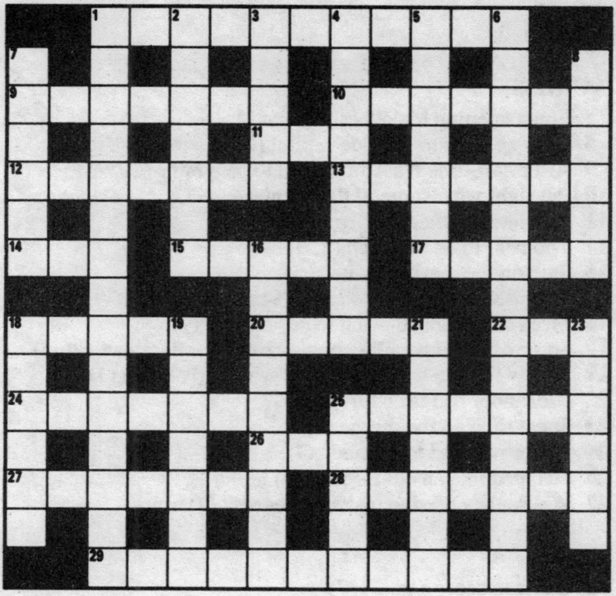

53

ACROSS

1 Fresh opening for old criminals (7)
5 Gear up so as to provide capital (6)
9 After half-time it's Anita's turn to be a fairy (7)
10 Put right what some of them finished (7)
11 A quietener after the fire (3)
12 Too near to be revealed (5, 6)
13 Ship on the marked route? (5)
14 Provided where there's room (9)
16 Tired of being subjected to car fumes? (9)
17 Some of those popular songs are quite inflammatory! (5)
19 All the time Len gets involved with party men (11)
22 Alexander had time for it (3)
23 Spent time on the throne (7)
24 Agreement not to expand? (7)
26 Stripped like an old Bobby? (6)
27 Where they used to make sixpences? (7)

DOWN

1 Game to score a goal? (7)
2 River time-keeping in Germany? (5, 2, 3, 5)
3 Name a heartless sister (3)
4 Time to identify poetic inspiration (5)
5 Such shares as one would rather have? (9)
6 Among the bad elements on the distaff side (5)
7 Having not yet emerged from the depths (5, 3, 7)
8 Prepared for the printer (6)
12 Island business ruffling the fur (5)
14 Foolish enough to increase one's size in hats? (3-6)
15 State of unrest among the laity (5)
16 Former wine business (6)
18 Time for the evening performance each day (7)
20 Cancel a rise for Sally the cake girl (5)
21 In diplomacy one leaves something unsaid (5)
25 The person in command (3)

54

ACROSS

1 Raising the burden of Olympic sport? (6-7)
8 Man of outstanding character? (4)
9 Some of you seem to have a purpose (3)
10 He gets professional advice as to his right in a small court (6)
11 Balls to the batsman (10)
13 I don't quite risk her appearance (4)
14 Room with a view (6)
16 Stick diagram into different hats (3-5)
19 He can't stay in the country (8)
22 Adder coiled round a circle in the tree (6)
25 Not quite top in Greek (4)
26 Business of a sailor who never goes to sea? (10)
27 Means of tying up a trail deviation (6)
28 Shoot in to a container (3)
29 Nothing included in honour of the instrument (4)
30 Tough-skinned grub? (7-6)

DOWN

1 A room we adapted to provide a range (7)
2 Breathe encouragement? (7)
3 It keeps a family afloat (5-4)
4 Not expected to an upright person? (3)
5 Loud performances not to be denied (5)
6 A letter of introduction (7)
7 Plant from neat gin (7)
12 Metaphor of the heathen temple? (7)
15 Move quickly to close the gap (3)
17 Handy gear to change in the shrubbery (9)
18 Help a girl who's lost her head (3)
20 One to one is visibly a confrontation! (7)
21 Nothing providing transport in a simple musical context (7)
23 The view from inside (7)
24 Down-to-earth business (7)
26 Being foreigners, they pay for themselves (5)
28 The drinking profession? (3)

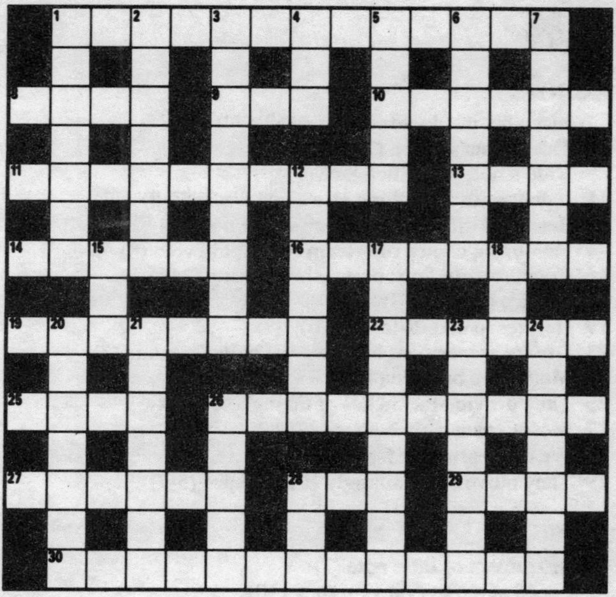
1
2
3
4
5
6
7
8
9
10
11
12
13
14
15
16
17
18
19
20
21
22
23
24
25
26
27
28
29
30

55

ACROSS

1 Just what the doctor ordered (12)
8 Takes what's given (7)
9 Hide a note on ruffled lace (7)
11 It goes with something else a girl wears (2-8)
12 Retreat is difficult when one's out on it (4)
14 Favouring choice of reform of the paid vote (8)
16 Concert including some rather hot stuff? (6)
17 Service garment (3)
19 He tries to end ill-feeling (6)
21 Dreary amusement has a way of being genuine (8)
24 Man in the balance (4)
25 They provide the means of taking a blow (4-6)
27 Most expensively beloved (7)
28 We can learn a lot from this (7)
29 They move entertainingly at the centre (5-7)

DOWN

1 Instrument of little note (7)
2 Speed of a party on a journey (10)
3 Great lover of Italy (8)
4 Encourage to make it nice for a change (6)
5 Container of fighting potential (4)
6 Memorial honour for adapting silk (7)
7 It was kept with vigilant protectiveness (5, 3, 4)
10 As a politician I celebrate what's enlightening (12)
13 It must be the mood! (10)
15 The little fellow is himself at last (3)
18 News of where the projectile entered? (8)
20 What a performance to give us the word! (7)
22 I don't like them to see mine scattered (7)
23 Went different ways for a bit? (6)
26 More than able to get at the truth satisfactorily? (4)

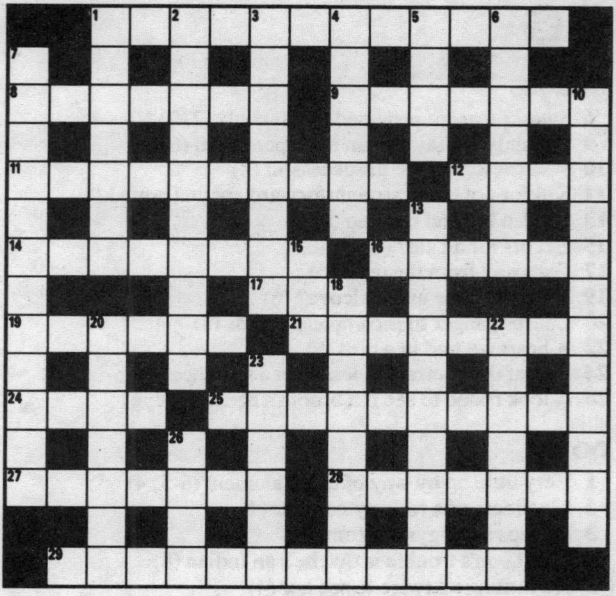

56

ACROSS

6 Sweet pleasure provided in Istanbul? (7, 7)
9 Grounds for having fun in Copenhagen (6)
10 Weaknesses of the unsuccessful (8)
11 Kill for not being straightforward about a pound (8)
13 Hidden beyond our ken (6)
15 Get off for an ale? (6)
17 Get away from the tents (6)
19 No work done in the alcove? (6)
20 Causes danger to incomplete beards (8)
22 A heart we find in a bird (8)
24 Part of the contract in less than a sentence (6)
26 A look round to see if a broom's needed? (8, 6)

DOWN

1 Very little on by way of entertainment (5-5, 4)
2 Liveliness of a railway number (4)
3 It keeps a clergyman going (6)
4 Half Leon's trouble is that he's an Indian (8)
5 I'm turning up twice to see her (4)
7 Blew when deprived of a draughtsman (6)
8 Looking very smart at the summit? (6, 8)
12 Fully conscious of a veil being fluttered (5)
14 It's taken to keep the meeting in order (5)
16 This year's trouble is excessive emotion (8)
18 It provides a boring time at sea (3-3)
21 Preserve a child in trouble! (6)
23 Summit meeting (4)
25 Farcical relative (4)

57

ACROSS

1 Leading for a short time among the trees (8)
5 Go about everything quietly but be quick! (6)
9 Scorn for an offence against the court (8)
10 Pretext for a new TV set? (6)
12 Nothing to write Frank (4)
13 Fools among the tangled reeds weighed up again (10)
15 They make living in sporting fashion (13)
19 Stop the flow of dance hits? (4, 3, 3, 3)
23 One of the tough old bosses? (4-6)
25 One-way transport for a striking opponent (4)
28 Ornamental gun? (6)
29 Soften one opening after a boy's return (8)
30 Cast a shadow on a vessel in the study (6)
31 Not knowing it's possibly not a ring (8)

DOWN

1 Agent to reckon with (6)
2 Scope for the mountaineer? (5)
3 Face motorway directions (4)
4 Prue's arrangement with me is best (7)
6 Having no companion makes a difference to Noel (5)
7 Be quick to acquire that edgy appearance? (4, 5)
8 He takes off in a funny way (8)
11 Invites to give information (4)
14 With the Scotsman away the wise man's on his own (4)
15 He doesn't just speak for our entertainment (9)
16 Ready to make a collection (3)
17 It's taken to indicate a true intention (4)
18 Tore off in the nude? (8)
20 Only one when it's doubled (4)
21 Having an inclination not to be on one's toes? (7)
22 The thing that causes protest? (6)
24 Creature causing some confusion round the ring (5)
26 She makes something of a declaration of love (5)
27 Oils blended in store (4)

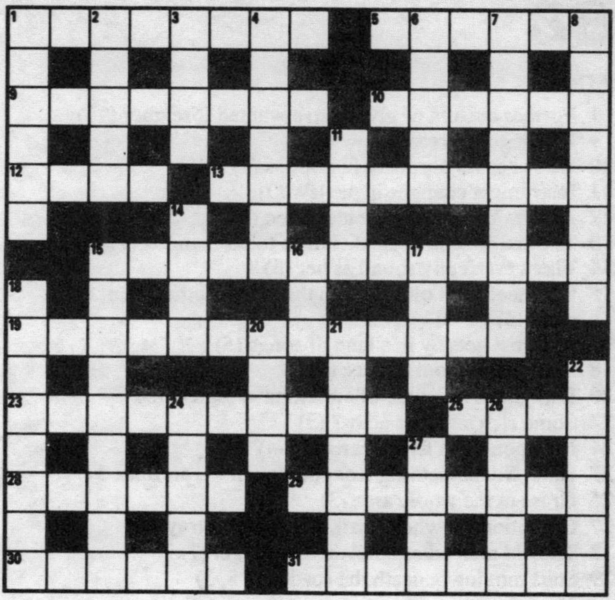

58

ACROSS

1 Former custom of giving up a wanted foreigner (11)
9 Privileged person in town (7)
10 He's at cross purposes in politics (7)
11 Instrument changes in the law (3)
12 A New York corpse unidentified (7)
13 They're done in coats that have to be changed (7)
14 There aren't any sound as her (3)
15 You need a bit of luck with the plain-clothes men, it's clear (5)
17 An artist gets by in a land of songs (5)
18 Ray's letter from Greece (5)
20 It might cover some of our embarrassment (5)
22 Some rich amateur actor? (3)
24 Low point in a flying career (3-4)
25 Hand Bill something from the tree if it's permitted (7)
26 Grass in the whole area (3)
27 Conditions in which mail, etc., goes astray (7)
28 The old man takes a boy in as a knight (7)
29 Start moving beneath the road? (3, 5, 3)

DOWN

1 When a maiden sings (5, 3, 7)
2 Work a brief reference in as a matter of form (7)
3 Try to test the metal (5)
4 Foreigner involved in a certain coolness (9)
5 It may keep you going but won't get you started (7)
6 Time off for that Aintree race? (8, 7)
7 Get on a bit oddly (6)
8 Irritable on the surface? (6)
16 Creature of colourful adaptability (9)
18 Look like a ricochet (6)
19 First man to find a worker unyielding (7)
21 Everything in entertainment lacks profundity (7)
23 Trapping the king into marriage? (6)
25 Goes round one way in error (5)

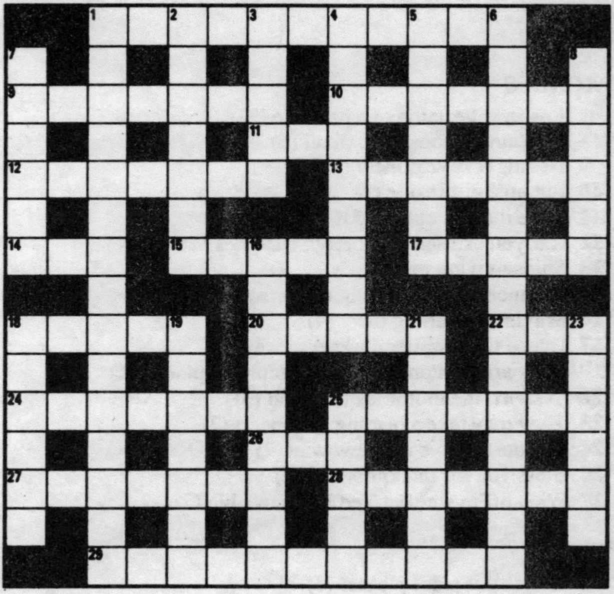

59

ACROSS

1 Lasting alteration of a bad rule (7)
5 Container deposit for alkali (6)
9 He might have done it (7)
10 Put up a girl inside (7)
11 Take it on an outing (3)
12 Car you can sell for foreign currency? (11)
13 Ships moving fast (5)
14 Defence occasion going on for some days (9)
16 Maxim for getting tick? (9)
17 Dance the summer darkness away (5)
19 They are outstanding as geographical plans (11)
22 In short, the motor is quite cold (3)
23 They may take a beating in concert (7)
24 Be constructive in a new way (7)
26 Bless you for that outburst! (6)
27 Went off to sort out Ted Ray's trouble (7)

DOWN

1 Ladies this side, please! (7)
2 It was his ghoulish business to raise the dead (12-3)
3 Creature in a crazy bonnet? (3)
4 Sent down to the interior (5)
5 The sort of shares one would rather have had (9)
6 After finishing it tear into the river (5)
7 In which a respectable front is maintained in patches? (6, 9)
8 Bond available for what little money there is about me (6)
12 Get hold of the song (5)
14 Painful experience of a TV personality with teeth (5-4)
15 Money for composition? (5)
16 Animal causing a depression in the Women's Institute (6)
18 Went too far as a top performer? (7)
20 Don't make contact with a girl about this time (5)
21 They may be much feared in progressive circles (5)
25 Keep out people who plead (3)

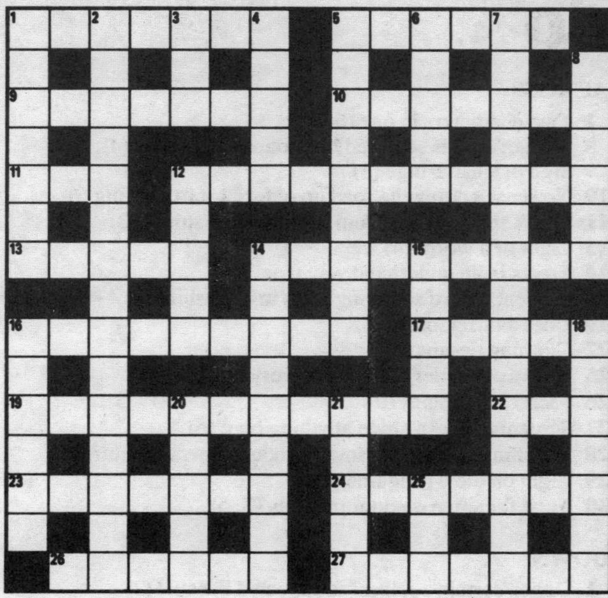
1 2 3 4 5 6 7 8 9 10 11 12 13 14 15 16 17 18 19 20 21 22 23 24 25 26 27

60

ACROSS

1 Two characters in one (6, 3, 4)
8 A lot of land is returned in a couple of articles (4)
9 Sign of a battering? (3)
10 No sense getting the road up before I start digging (6)
11 Enid's spray comes from the medicine store (10)
13 Light of a worm (4)
14 Erects in an underhand way (6)
16 Prudent record sounding right in Yorkshire (8)
19 Does a turn loosely (8)
22 Clothing tie-up (6)
25 Note a container that may be very hot (4)
26 Secret boldness? (10)
27 Screening doesn't hide anything here (6)
28 Welshman given one small announcement in return (3)
29 Right on the wrong line (4)
30 Time for some outdoor pursuits (7, 6)

DOWN

1 Only a certain coolness is expected in court (7)
2 Flinty character making the hard breaks (7)
3 It may be held to improve the vision (9)
4 Connection to hand (3)
5 Not so if it's any good (5)
6 Elder follower (7)
7 Happening to be part of a TV serial, possibly (7)
12 Don's aid is the making of a writer (7)
15 Edible island (3)
17 Make allowances for a protêgê (9)
18 East or West, the last of London (3)
20 Feed in hours of confusion (7)
21 Business worry? (7)
23 Points of Chinese medicine (7)
24 Basis for Bible reading (7)
26 Cover one creature (5)
28 Appreciate in depth? (3)

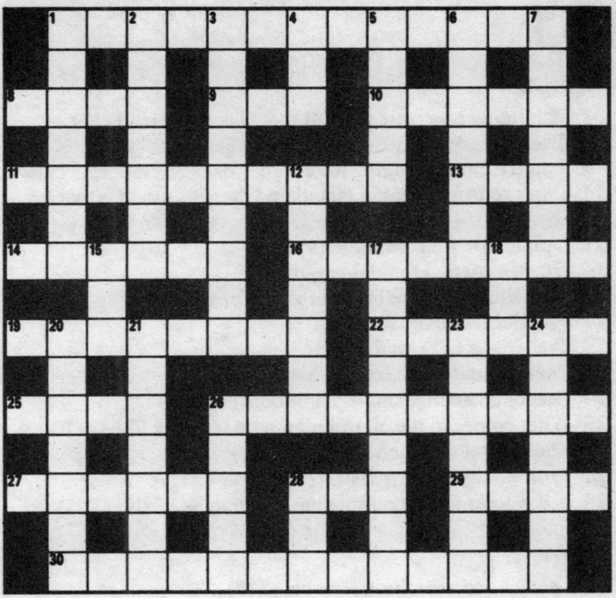
1 2 3 4 5 6 7
8 9 10
11 12 13
14 15 16 17 18
19 20 21 22 23 24
25 26
27 28 29
30

61

ACROSS

1 Belonging to a page in print that was misplaced (12)
8 They sound painfully dissatisfied (7)
9 Top Irishman bringing a foreigner back to elaborate (7)
11 Clear return to Rhode Island and then all round America – absurd! (10)
12 Opinion of what's visible (4)
14 Grudge carried to fatal lengths (8)
16 Tom the adventure book hero can be quite cutting (6)
17 Wander in Dover Road (3)
19 See what a CID man does (6)
21 Tear around in a haze and handle badly (8)
24 One of those dressing-up numbers (4)
25 What comes to the churchman who is better liked? (10)
27 The habitat in which one thrives (7)
28 Fruit finally causing a fuss (7)
29 Is it fought when one side has taken to its heels? (7, 5)

DOWN

1 Leave a radio orchestra playing? (7)
2 Knowledge of coming changes in price scene (10)
3 Determined to turn the unsuccessful one up first (8)
4 More difficult for a Cockney to indicate enthusiasm? (6)
5 Blue service (4)
6 Its absolutely nothing! (7)
7 A claim to be God shows lack of foresight (12)
10 Centre of current affairs (5, 7)
13 Quick talk with notes added can be an entertaining ditty (6-4)
15 It may be upheld to cause a stoppage (3)
18 Undesirables in a North African air force starting a fight (4-4)
20 It's open at the back of the car (7)
22 Get lean so as to look smart (7)
23 Just a little bit in favour of a heavyweight (6)
26 Head chap? (4)

62

ACROSS

6 Royal person who sought a relationship on a special footing (6, 8)
9 You can't be sure you'll win it (6)
10 No occasion for generosity between events? (8)
11 Ask Barnaby to show envy (8)
13 Jack being packed off isn't here (6)
15 Fight on points that could be scanty (6)
17 Shiver of excitement (6)
19 Get on with it, understand? (6)
20 The expense of a hat? (8)
22 It could just happen (8)
24 Person of drive able to get round the doctor's organisation (6)
26 Formation of Musketeers, for instance? (6, 8)

DOWN

1 Scene of gas leakage near Marble Arch (8, 6)
2 Trunk attachment (4)
3 Writing to show the way to one's beliefs (6)
4 A place for science in the money vessel (8)
5 Something dirty that turns small stomachs (4)
7 Wave to put hair in order? (6)
8 They don't do the successful litigant's name any good! (7, 7)
12 Respond with more drama (5)
14 Man of metal (5)
16 Cut some land in Tyne and Wear? (8)
18 Liable to die like an ordinary person (6)
21 His propositions can be put to the proof (6)
23 Warriors, some limping away (4)
25 Source of money on the side? (4)

1
2
3
4
5
6
7
8
9
10
11
12
13
14
15
16
17
18
19
20
21
22
23
24
25
26

63

ACROSS

1 Bankrupt swimmer with a limp? (4, 4)
5 City exchange all at sea, apparently (6)
9 Wholesome greeting? (8)
10 Good man ending prayer with a bit of a bloomer (6)
12 Morris men's number (4)
13 Does it cause a certain coolness on pay day? (4, 6)
15 Money you don't let fall from your grasp! (7, 2, 4)
19 Taking in all at school (13)
23 Tempting morsel stuck in the throat? (5, 5)
25 Sporting Freddie's unmanned, there's no denying (4)
28 Objection to weight in a fastener (6)
29 Something's wrong here! (8)
30 Coster knocked about by someone with him (6)
31 Ray's come to make trouble in the wood (8)

DOWN

1 Unsuccessful offence in the record (6)
2 Look among people signifying something juicy (5)
3 There's an obligation to pay it (4)
4 Cover up the end of the show (7)
6 Some of that defilement that comes from Rose (5)
7 Mate Peter nobbled without going to extremes (9)
8 Argues certain conclusions after starting to contradict (8)
11 This is the place to give the girl direction (4)
14 It's not clearly uncomplimentary (4)
15 Like that inflated talk about IRA activity? (9)
16 Take this for a start! (3)
17 It may take a hammering (4)
18 Quick! Prepare the eggs (8)
20 Eternal springer (4)
21 Nothing you can find translated in Tully (7)
22 Education to some extent (6)
24 Old Bob may not be rich but, perhaps, has a follower (5)
26 A riot put into proportion (5)
27 Facts of Canada taxes (4)

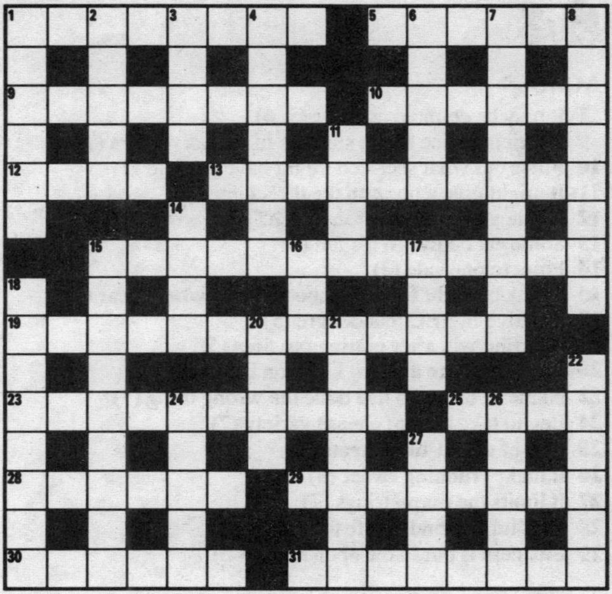
1
2
3
4
5
6
7
8
9
10
11
12
13
14
15
16
17
18
19
20
21
22
23
24
25
26
27
28
29
30
31

64

ACROSS

1 It may be counted as error (5, 6)
9 Linking device found suitable in road diversion (7)
10 Finds out what sect Ted might have got into (7)
11 It might give a buzz on the direct line (3)
12 Do they give instruction to fish? (7)
13 Some err badly, so it's felt (7)
14 Point to one side (3)
15 Trunk brought from Bagshot or somewhere near (5)
17 Relative in EEC manoeuvre (5)
18 Sporting win after putting out fires (5)
20 In which there are two kings on board (5)
22 Name of one who had done the wrong thing (3)
24 Beg to take note of cheese variety (7)
25 One of the all-time greats (7)
26 It makes running easier (3)
27 It limits the outpourings (7)
28 Ian's turn to find a wife to inspire (7)
29 Business is out in the open here (6-5)

DOWN

1 Survive big trouble in wind and rain (7, 3, 5)
2 Mail despatched to a remote station? (7)
3 Provides personal cover (5)
4 Yet fully cooked at the bottom (9)
5 He may be in the running after a hit (7)
6 As has been said before, you may get it if you call an absent friend (8, 7)
7 Hound some fool into a gamble (6)
8 Member of a sect way beyond a German town (6)
16 Mount to reach Rose by a roundaboout route (9)
18 It's surprisingly hostile (6)
19 Coach below the line? (7)
21 Tina and Sam have what it takes to keep going (7)
23 Working man who may cut things short (6)
25 Hold on to a decoration (5)

1 2 3 4 5 6 7 8 9 10 11 12 13 14 15 16 17 18 19 20 21 22 23 24 25 26 27 28 29

65

ACROSS

1 Absolutely right after so much practice! (7)
5 Governing course for getting insurance in writing (6)
9 Song about a rotter in a happy land (7)
10 Bad turn giving some indication of a food centre (7)
11 Advice to give money (3)
12 Conditioned by clean thinking? (11)
13 Little one given a hood in time (5)
14 It just shows what's going to happen (9)
16 Nice grant dissipated quickly on a horse (9)
17 Makes a cross decision (5)
19 As sensational as an optician's work? (11)
22 Make a dash for it (3)
23 Where the rock is seen to cut even more? (7)
24 Medicinal gum resin (7)
26 Could the girl be disturbed by a pet? (6)
27 Indication of a nation's prickliness? (7)

DOWN

1 Smooth stuff that may make the cat slip (7)
2 Where one might be taken in for a party? (9, 6)
3 This is it at last! (3)
4 It gives a lady high-level glitter (5)
5 It doesn't reach the musical heights in church (5-4)
6 Girl from the old country (5)
7 Settle down, Cock, when schemes recoil on you (4, 4, 2, 5)
8 Nervous about indulging in brinkmanship? (2, 4)
12 It shows you belong (5)
14 It's the top man that attracts interest (9)
15 He gets around the dog! (5)
16 One of the twins can give you sugar (6)
18 Possibly nicer in the South-East, to be honest (7)
20 Movement stirs the broth (5)
21 Come down for some clarification (5)
25 Girl with no study – she's probably foreign (3)

1
2
3
4
5
6
7
8
9
10
11
12
13
14
15
16
17
18
19
20
21
22
23
24
25
26
27

66

ACROSS

1 How one might be doubly grasping (4, 4, 5)
8 She's carried back and forth by the Canadian National Railway (4)
9 Vessel of some grandeur, naturally (3)
10 Heavenly appearance of the sex appeal revolution (6)
11 The secret of trust (10)
13 Port goes to Tom's head and there's trouble! (4)
14 Save and possibly make secure (6)
16 Given shape by the girl in the studio? (8)
19 Emphasised a new look in the dress set (8)
22 It enables one to go below (6)
25 Weapons brought back into the bar (4)
26 Unknown river for writers (10)
27 Talk about a flier in the river! (6)
28 Eggs getting some approval (3)
29 Fall down on the journey (4)
30 Can't be given effect before an uncle comes round (13)

DOWN

1 Partly successful in seeming pleasant (7)
2 Do business in passing? (7)
3 Big enough not to jump so much (9)
4 Taking part in getting money (3)
5 It's made to get there quicker (5)
6 True note of a simpleton (7)
7 He appreciated Christmas in the end (7)
12 Not likely to make a settlement (7)
15 Dear man of letters (3)
17 Deep in tears in hopeless disarray (9)
18 Sound rather down (3)
20 Car part for one aunt (7)
21 Make a deep impression as a designer (7)
23 Dip in here for the present (4-3)
24 By which travel can be put down to overheads? (3-4)
26 One isn't wanted on it (5)
28 It's put in to interfere (3)

67

ACROSS

1 Can they restore ailing religions? (5, 7)
8 Add tape that may be changed (7)
9 Woollies for two? (4-3)
11 Something to be gained by working for a time (10)
12 Move to bring our favourites back (4)
14 Unnecessary embellishment (8)
16 Finished the journey without conviction? (3, 3)
17 Saw a comeback that happened to be (3)
19 Sounds like a chap with bronchitis – it's the chest (6)
21 Send a resort into depression (8)
24 Container for a weapon of war? (4)
25 Officer helping to put up a tent in France? (4-2-4)
27 Many said to have a fear of Germans (7)
28 Nominal start (7)
29 Faint possibility of getting far away? (6, 6)

DOWN

1 Flighty young thing (7)
2 Moved in to adopt what could be re-invented (10)
3 Line-up between the fields (8)
4 Lure out of an apprenticeship (6)
5 Retreat from a rail diversion (4)
6 Almost risk a foreigner for something to eat (7)
7 Whisky matter heard in an Edinburgh court, for instance? (4, 2, 6)
10 In a position to claim a seat (3, 2, 3, 4)
13 We may achieve this when all's said and done (10)
15 The miser keeps it tight (3)
18 You haven't got this on your plate (4-4)
20 Money can be changed in splendid surroundings (7)
22 It might cause a stoppage after lunch (3-4)
23 The sex that's extinct in local government (6)
26 After some hesitation departure can be deduced (4)

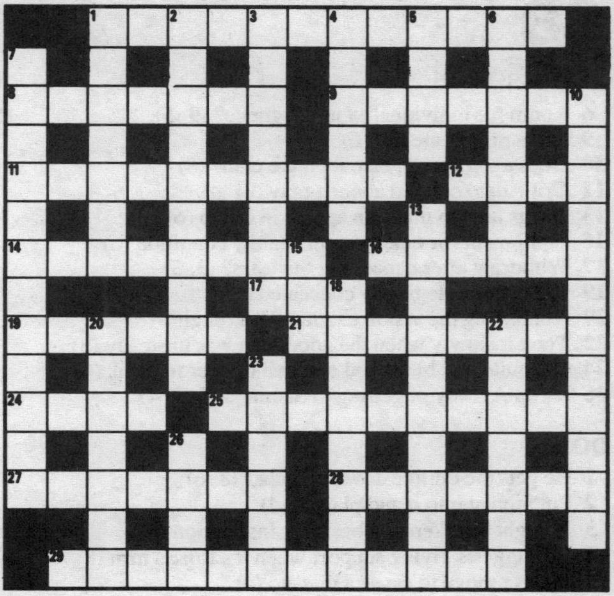
1
2
3
4
5
6
7
8
9
10
11
12
13
14
15
16
17
18
19
20
21
22
23
24
25
26
27
28
29

68

ACROSS

6 Room for individuality in a vignette? (9, 5)
9 Not a proper ale run (6)
10 Does a top person take it on the chin? (8)
11 Crit Adam offered about a play (8)
13 Twigs how to make an appeal in a ship (6)
15 Equipment for emerging in healthy condition (6)
17 Withdraw after cancelling the tears? (3, 3)
19 Flower or note finally concealed (6)
20 Not having the vision to adapt U.S. engine (8)
22 Took it slowly when the good man was unsteady (8)
24 One mild and bitter and one half of beer to drink (6)
26 It's an A1 way of getting to Scotland (5, 5, 4)

DOWN

1 He gets the outline down on paper (8, 6)
2 Put money into it and play it! (4)
3 It might be taken as a basis for inscription (6)
4 He suggests giving support when it's Rose's turn (8)
5 Make a move to cause a mix-up (4)
7 Move like a hag at wit's end (6)
8 Classic contrast to the VIP's journal (5, 2, 1, 6)
12 May set light to some correspondence (5)
14 Peer's son in the Sappers in France (5)
16 Nine told not to be hard workers (8)
18 Fatal result of raising a coloured drink (6)
21 Thin excuse for taking offence? (6)
23 Give a ring to a girl displaying the shape (4)
25 Volume of betting (4)

1
2
3
4
5
6
7
8
9
10
11
12
13
14
15
16
17
18
19
20
21
22
23
24
25
26

69

ACROSS

1 'You may telephone from here,' for instance? (4, 4)
5 It's easy if you're rich! (6)
9 Take a French husband for a period by the sea (8)
10 Serviceman to join when I leave (6)
12 Things get heated here (4)
13 For those afraid to make a dash behind the wire? (7-3)
15 Make official mention of the disc label address? (5, 2, 6)
19 Show how the story might look if concealed? (6, 7)
23 Noel's merit looks different in town (10)
25 Father Kelly's origins aren't real (4)
28 Pictures for which a gem is exchanged (6)
29 There's trouble when matters aren't straightened out (8)
30 Quite a packet! (6)
31 He doesn't know how to mix Ascot gin (8)

DOWN

1 Often seen on the land (6)
2 Great Elgar variation (5)
3 Peace that passeth understanding includes him (4)
4 Does it stick to one's foot? (7)
6 They're over there (5)
7 Duck below for warmth (5-4)
8 Dot and Henry in a lamentable entanglement (8)
11 Look at broken cans (4)
14 Payment to conduct war? (4)
15 A chap needs time if he's important (9)
16 A person you could finally reach by telephone (3)
17 Very bad in Seville (4)
18 David, for instance, confused his pals with poor visibility (8)
20 Undercover (4)
21 Winding in a fish caught in the circle (7)
22 Poetic system of measurement? (6)
24 Clumsy enclosure set up in it (5)
26 Check on the college ale (5)
27 More than one can play it (4)

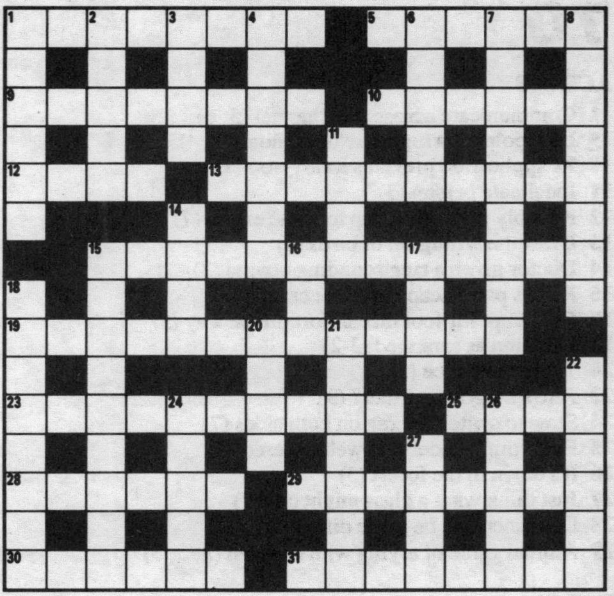

70

ACROSS

1 Communicate across the Channel (5, 6)
9 Low point of a high-rise operation? (3, 4)
10 Its application prevents a carry-on (7)
11 Indelicate person (3)
12 Possibly giving it a slap to some extent (7)
13 Draw the wrong set of birds (7)
14 Doctor given a ring sounding bovine (3)
15 Pearl's parent can move the crane (5)
17 Contempt for foot discomfort on the way (5)
18 Situation as arranged (3-2)
20 Table of service (5)
22 Pete's no-good partner? (3)
24 Slow to switch the rag on both sides (7)
25 Everything under it is well ordered (7)
26 It's down in the forest (3)
27 Just think what a glass might do! (7)
28 Dead men can be made different (7)
29 Animal game of toying with a victim (3, 3, 5)

DOWN

1 Liquid movement that might set into jam? (6, 2, 7)
2 An excuse to be avoided? (7)
3 Get down to make a high appeal (5)
4 Somebody's given him a bundle of nice tripe (9)
5 Sold one that's broken to the fools (7)
6 She does too much domestic work (9, 6)
7 Good-looking, sound old vehicle (6)
8 I'm first! (6)
16 He can't be relied on to burn the French brown (9)
18 Ray and Gus in sweet confusion (6)
19 Sensible girl making an impression (7)
21 Our dean can be quite poetic! (7)
23 Fool the king in the river (6)
25 Charles Morgan briefly yawning (5)

71

ACROSS

1 Take away newspapers to cause gloom? (7)
5 Related to the breed (6)
9 Put me back in the box and burn it (7)
10 There's a chance he could win (7)
11 Time for only half the business of the meeting (3)
12 Wrongly I call parson a mean creature (11)
13 The family gang (5)
14 Film sponsor? (9)
16 Entertains when on edge during bookish sessions (9)
17 Charming notes having a soothing effect (5)
19 Taken in by a conversion to something very like (11)
22 Cause of many a work stoppage (3)
23 Approve a decision to study the business (7)
24 Our future is in our own hands, he thinks (7)
26 It flows always between poles (6)
27 Cause amazement at different times? (7)

DOWN

1 Cancel a request to recite (7)
2 Rubbish composition in part? (5, 2, 8)
3 Intemperate time (3)
4 They may be counted with closed eyes (5)
5 The monarchy is fatally affected by them (9)
6 Animal with penetrating eye trouble (5)
7 When MPs are too tired to stand up and speak? (3-5, 7)
8 One is included among foreign coins (6)
12 They give support to those who are going places (5)
14 Not tough enough to be cads? (9)
15 Given strength by a distorted dream (5)
16 Leave the trunk at Bull's Head farm (6)
18 Talk of the century taking on a mad character (7)
20 Most important way to identify a state (5)
21 Records certain tie-ups (5)
25 Jump quietly away in the grass (3)

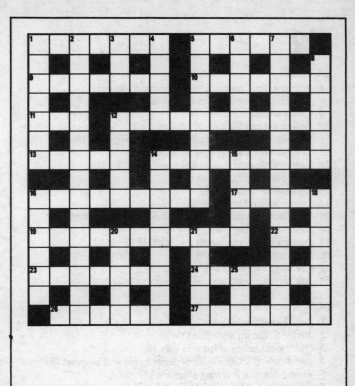

72

ACROSS

1 Pass the pipe, perhaps, to make one (5-8)
8 To her, the way appears in Scotland (4)
9 Cover a team member (3)
10 Before the big fight (3-3)
11 Cinema clue to reforms embracing Christians (10)
13 Top man for a short time in Africa (4)
14 Convertible dealer who has got ahead (6)
16 Incorporated in the flesh (8)
19 Crossed in outlook? (8)
22 Canter around in a daze (6)
25 On which one might take it without dodging trouble (4)
26 Agree in writing (10)
27 Decoration in a payment fix, it's said (6)
28 Light round the bend (3)
29 Crossing supporter (4)
30 Are its judgments specially attractive? (5, 2, 6)

DOWN

1 Deal harshly with what's painful in style (7)
2 Afraid to cut up a medlar (7)
3 Quite a character in his odd way (9)
4 Just dandy if a Government department will be quiet (3)
5 Throw out of a learning situation (5)
6 Where the cold war might be short of a pound (7)
7 Tearing around can be very hard (7)
12 He and the divine get in a vehicle in Somerset (7)
15 Liable to be the fastest on the line one day (3)
17 Fat container in flowery form (9)
18 Caledonian John (3)
20 Morning for a rich change of language (7)
21 One aunt shaken up in the back of the car (7)
23 Soften the old man up with some pudding (7)
24 Expecting the worst of people (7)
26 Treasury located in a revolutionary thoroughfare (5)
28 Great chap losing colour (3)

1 2 3 4 5 6 7 8 9 10 11 12 13 14 15 16 17 18 19 20 21 22 23 24 25 26 27 28 29 30

73

ACROSS

6 Equalise the weight in the shop scales? (14)
9 Sound agreement (6)
10 Quite the moment for getting up? (4, 4)
11 Mum suffocates in the ship (8)
13 Ask in quick French (6)
15 Not too stupid to get an angle? (6)
17 Tea permitted in the house (6)
19 A whiff of the way to the top (6)
20 Went into haberdashery years ago (8)
22 It could give a girl cover till a man comes round (8)
24 He tries to promote better feelings (6)
26 Practise retaining an inner grip (4, 4, 4, 2)

DOWN

1 The bigger the cheaper when it comes to covering fish? (7, 2, 5)
2 Creature booted into the theatre (4)
3 Enacts a change of position (6)
4 Droop like Lydia on the stage (8)
5 It's no fancy matter! (4)
7 Put the girl up on top of the tree in new form (6)
8 Taper, stop rambling! (4, 2, 3, 5)
12 Article follows after turning it up in part (5)
14 Little Virginia allowed to be a servant (5)
16 Paying up or sinking down (8)
18 They may contribute to dress upkeep (6)
21 Make popular at last with the listener (6)
23 Work at a keyboard of a kind (4)
25 Rules for preserving security? (4)

74

ACROSS

1 Change one franc or five hundred in a TV town (8)
5 Stop an artist going back with the others (6)
9 Song of the outsider (8)
10 Sorry state of an engagement (6)
12 Little Dickensian (4)
13 Express regret about one that will lose value (10)
15 Ground for a striking encounter (5, 2, 6)
19 Moving around with blood? (2, 11)
23 Not oppressed by being in space? (10)
25 All-round personality of the Gulf area (4)
28 Fruit of petty republicanism (6)
29 Quicker to damage the jetty? (8)
30 Sign for service (6)
31 Get home without me this way! (8)

DOWN

1 Examining the joint on the outside (6)
2 Time for fools at first (5)
3 Discover the devil to be heartless (4)
4 Mr Brezhnev, William Rufus? (7)
6 All that's left of poor Eric around fifty (5)
7 Edward puts his country before a Villa in the Midlands (9)
8 Moved towards a fall (8)
11 Zeppelin, for instance, of note to British fliers (4)
14 Be tolerant of a beast (4)
15 Imagined by a writer (9)
16 Pussy's boating companion (3)
17 Girl shown as about six (4)
18 May be seen as capable of surviving when we turn up inside (8)
20 Like panto sisters (4)
21 It may be noted when one isn't seen (7)
22 Girl in the network (6)
24 Depends on the capital punishment? (5)
26 I roam about for the girl (5)
27 Notice a point (4)

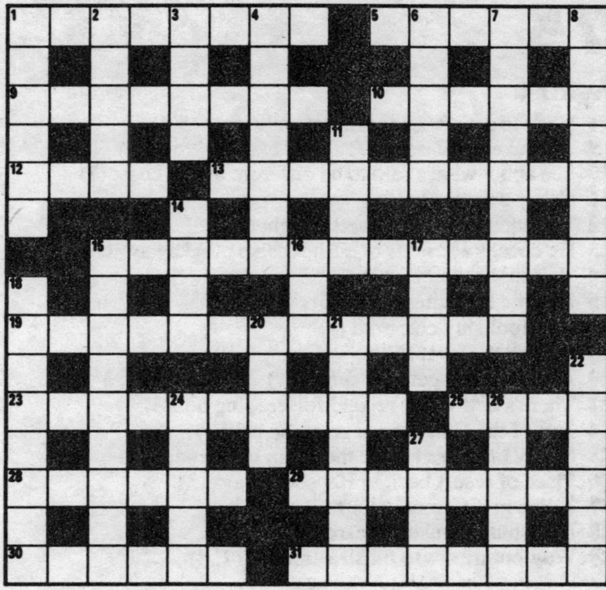

75

ACROSS

1 Keen to act after a theatrical walk-out? (5-6)
9 Ape an ecclesiastic? (7)
10 See about what's said to be different on the coast (7)
11 Crazy twister (3)
12 The squad that never gets it right (7)
13 He checks accounts of a Rhodesian breakaway summit (7)
14 He's in the welfare (3)
15 A name for being lordly (5)
17 He's foolishly cornered (5)
18 Hen on the level (5)
20 An eye for dispensing spirits (5)
22 There's nothing to be said for keeping her (3)
24 Part of the fruity message of the bells (7)
25 Funny business before the claim is amended (7)
26 Place of resort back in Hapsburg days (3)
27 A line in different colour (7)
28 Distributing business cards? (7)
29 Way-out means to finish a smoke? (7, 4)

DOWN

1 Explosive rod? (5, 2, 8)
2 Very firm man taking on a worker (7)
3 Correct some of them at last (5)
4 Old or new it's in the Book (9)
5 The girl died troubled by herself (7)
6 It might come a purler when power is applied (8-7)
7 Understanding subject of quick thinking (6)
8 Some measure of the educated man's angle? (6)
16 Use a tour to assemble an outfit (9)
18 Used to clean spectacles in the wrong half (6)
19 Mischievous use of the GI's hour (7)
21 Scot turning up with an almost capital drink (7)
23 Bad chief in Spain (6)
25 Bill and Edward turn up for a trainee (5)

76

ACROSS

1 He argues that the players include one among us (7)
5 Holder of a cricket trophy? (3-3)
9 Where one might learn to dispose of a red one (7)
10 He moves the goods (7)
11 He needs skill to communicate (3)
12 Liberal thinking about American women? (5-6)
13 Growing amusement with a soldier (5)
14 Infamous refusal to take port with us (9)
16 Like marauders dropped by Cockneys (9)
17 Doomed to suffer a deft redistribution (5)
19 Besides relating payment to distance travelled? (11)
22 Make a proprietorial disclosure (3)
23 All under it is in order (7)
24 The girl turning Bert's head is so effervescent! (7)
26 Wanting more of the man in discreet charcoal (6)
27 You'll do well to replace one who's gone (7)

DOWN

1 Communication if Fred begins in the city (7)
2 Dozing businessman (8, 7)
3 Part of the price freeze (3)
4 Music adds nothing to the flavour (5)
5 Hateful remedies? (9)
6 Given time I could become a dream girl (5)
7 Rashly invited bother (5, 3, 7)
8 They're modest yet improper in addition (6)
12 Pipe plant (5)
14 Aunt upset at the gathering, of course (9)
15 Plunder widespread around Leatherhead (5)
16 Move to make a pretence (6)
18 Not dead, given new form (7)
20 Can you see the crowd in such order? (5)
21 Caravanners stop here (5)
25 And a hundred more, shortly unspecified? (3)

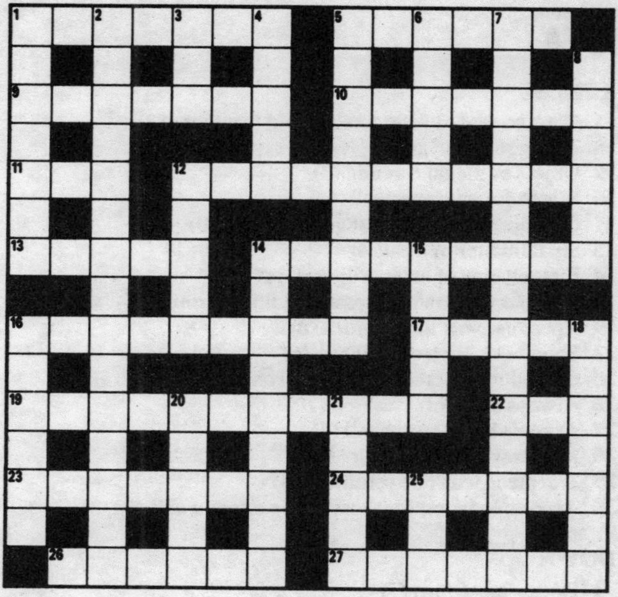

77

ACROSS

1 Can't be said to refer to some old trousers (13)
8 A singer at last! (4)
9 Object of illegal running (3)
10 Watch for a vegetarian? (6)
11 Certain evil in a bet that goes wrong (10)
13 Small matter of a cat (4)
14 First change of air in Yugoslavia (6)
16 Ran and put down a card after taking a round (8)
19 Apes Jean in a foreign turn (8)
22 Solid basis for a touchdown (6)
25 Capital return from Blackpool song contest (4)
26 Always in faithful fashion (10)
27 At one's best one can tell (6)
28 Its driver gets by with it (3)
29 The place won't be reformed (4)
30 Accommodation for those going straight up? (10, 3)

DOWN

1 Does a loose turn (7)
2 Digger appearing about four in a fur (7)
3 Vision of Black Bess? (9)
4 One article for a Scot (3)
5 Chemical inter-mixture (5)
6 Express disapproval of service accommodation? (7)
7 It happens to be part of the serial (7)
12 One bird attacked another (7)
15 Advice to dump (3)
17 Easily upset by misplaced tribal ire (9)
18 An ass, perhaps, that has to be obeyed (3)
20 Jack's devious hint to provide a drink (7)
21 Lax loot distribution among the amphibians (7)
23 Always carrying on (3-4)
24 Permitted to amend the dole law (7)
26 Funny business with Mickey losing the opener! (5)
28 Topping award for a chosen player! (3)

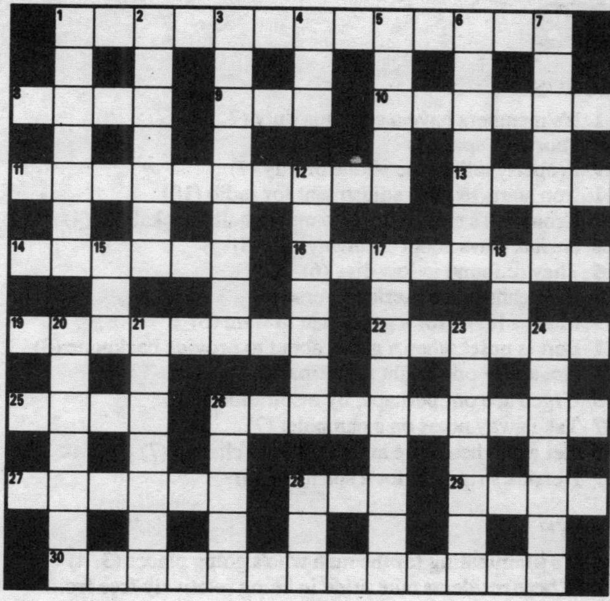
1
2
3
4
5
6
7
8
9
10
11
12
13
14
15
16
17
18
19
20
21
22
23
24
25
26
27
28
29
30

78

ACROSS

1 It's members have a common duty (7, 5)
8 Shorten a span (7)
9 Property talk in the phone briefly (7)
11 Iron starts to need adjustment for radio (10)
12 Cromwell's contribution to music-hall knockabout (4)
14 He has news about a railwayman (8)
16 They're found in low digs (6)
17 By means of a material reverse (3)
19 Made a home for a good man in want (6)
21 Bert is upset when a girl is about to provide backbone (8)
24 Not stuffy one might say offhand (4)
25 Urged ace on, perhaps, by inspiration (10)
27 Take away notes on a pamphlet (7)
28 Get wet when there are no times to change (7)
29 Herrick's ripe cry for a spirit? (6, 6)

DOWN

1 It's illuminating for the man who's going places (3, 4)
2 Where residents take pride in being relatively free from traffic? (4, 6)
3 Go beyond the mark (8)
4 Part mad coster (6)
5 Such a thing could be almost disastrous (4)
6 Push forward in the last offensive (7)
7 Having a grasp of the immediate business? (6, 2, 4)
10 Well-established claim to be seated? (4-8)
13 Give tin to Doris for twisting (10)
15 Clergyman going round shortly (3)
18 He wants to make a better arrangement (8)
20 Period to exercise the muscles (7)
22 Misplaced zeal of the great Tory revolution (7)
23 Like the problem of putting network together? (6)
26 Complementary couple (4)

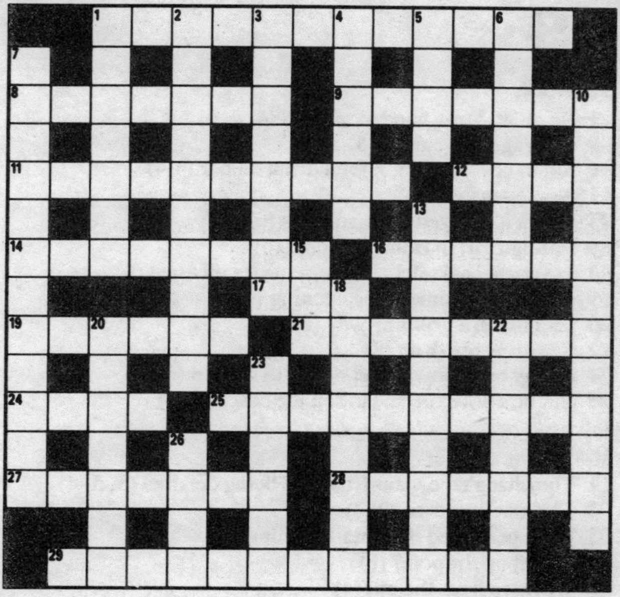
1
2
3
4
5
6
7
8
9
10
11
12
13
14
15
16
17
18
19
20
21
22
23
24
25
26
27
28
29

79

ACROSS

1 Be quiet – put hand to mouth? (4, 4, 6)
9 Ring again to cancel (6)
10 Ski in new formation for a drink holder (4-4)
11 No yes-man! (8)
13 When it's played the man turns (6)
15 Foreign girl in riding accident (6)
17 Do come back, debt notes are never pleasant (6)
19 Coming this time at the opening (6)
20 End life in a gripping way (8)
22 See drips break up (8)
24 It may be pressed to set things in motion (6)
26 But he's not expected to sell the cargo (8, 6)

DOWN

1 They hadn't the vision to avoid being detailed (5, 5, 4)
2 Obscene sportsman? (4)
3 Look permitted in a small opening (6)
4 Model up the pole? (8)
5 Workers from the hill (4)
7 The way to the stars (6)
8 World-famous dive offering many different turns? (9, 5)
12 Flier under par (5)
14 Rose has a point here (5)
16 It describes what outsiders may not see (8)
18 A whiff on the way up (6)
21 It may take away from one's writing (6)
23 A little kiss that could mean a lot (4)
25 As far as I'm concerned it's just a book (4)

80

ACROSS

1 Time to start a new day (8)
5 Clean inside the vessel that gives bad beer (6)
9 Water-colour? (8)
10 Communist vehicle to Yorkshire? (6)
12 Thought of an extract from 'Pride and Prejudice' (4)
13 No credit is involved in showing prudence (10)
15 Honestly refusing to be diverted (5, 8)
19 Does it enable you to see when things are rough? (9-4)
23 Settling into depressed circumstances (10)
25 Space for a small port? (4)
28 Speak evil of land on the Great Northern (6)
29 It puts one in the picture (8)
30 Given a hammering to prevent further movement (6)
31 Just a little entertainment on TV? (4-4)

DOWN

1 Decoration of the law? (6)
2 Man leaving the plant as a seaman (5)
3 Some small measure of personal expansion (4)
4 Mad enough for work among the vines? (7)
6 A question of position (5)
7 Choosing sides for improvement (7, 2)
8 Tranquility of poor Ernie in bad accommodation (8)
11 He has land in the North (4)
14 Soldier repeatedly identifying the film girl (4)
15 Italian patriot seen at teatime? (9)
16 Not a day for working (3)
17 Somewhat unbalanced personality (4)
18 He may be on the board (8)
20 A study in port (4)
21 Put in nearby after getting points (7)
22 Give the most satisfying cry (6)
24 Fire one some way away (5)
26 The noise of opposition (5)
27 Don't go on a street mission (4)

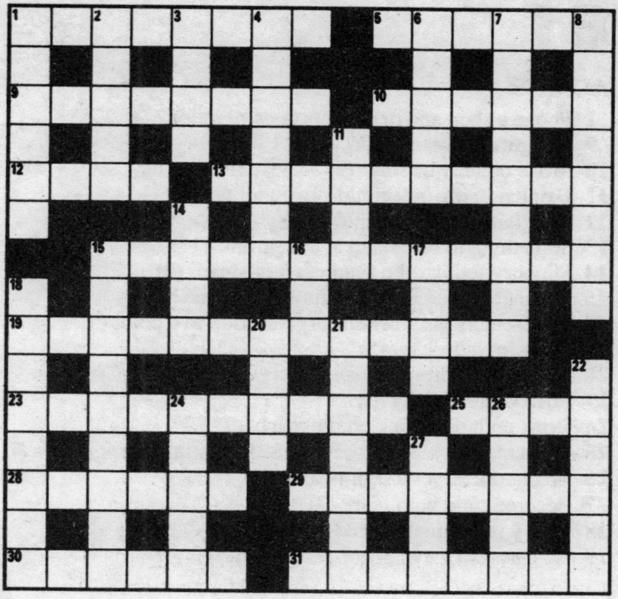

81

ACROSS

1 Phone a shop and demand proper attention? (4, 2, 5)
9 Delights of abstraction? (7)
10 Move quickly or sink! (7)
11 Drink nothing in teetotal surroundings (3)
12 Nice fan convertible into money (7)
13 Something to be gained at the entrance (7)
14 Slippery fellow, the headless huntsman! (3)
15 Somewhat mercurial institution in Rome (5)
17 He instructs the workers' organisation to a point (5)
18 Fight for a little bit (5)
20 Nice and wholesome (5)
22 Point of generosity (3)
24 Don't do it with Jack on the mark! (7)
25 Met a setback with a troublesome fellow in great agitation (7)
26 Much of it is of no significance (3)
27 Become rigid with fear? (7)
28 Heavy individual turn of ours (7)
29 Is he never free of proof-reading (6-5)

DOWN

1 A move into Europe (7, 8)
2 Not saying much about the French section, maybe (7)
3 State upheaval sensation! (5)
4 Set in boast awkwardly and not to be moved (9)
5 Sedative to obtain when on the floor, perhaps (7)
6 Fundamentally like one of the bad apples? (6, 2, 3, 4)
7 Suppress what is felt to be different (6)
8 He takes a cutting view of what's written (6)
16 Sound non-crease arrangement (9)
18 Fight on points for meagre result (6)
19 Having fun with a full-pay transfer (7)
21 Office bird of passage having time for colour (7)
23 Alkali in the urn? (6)
25 They are blamed by a bad workman (5)

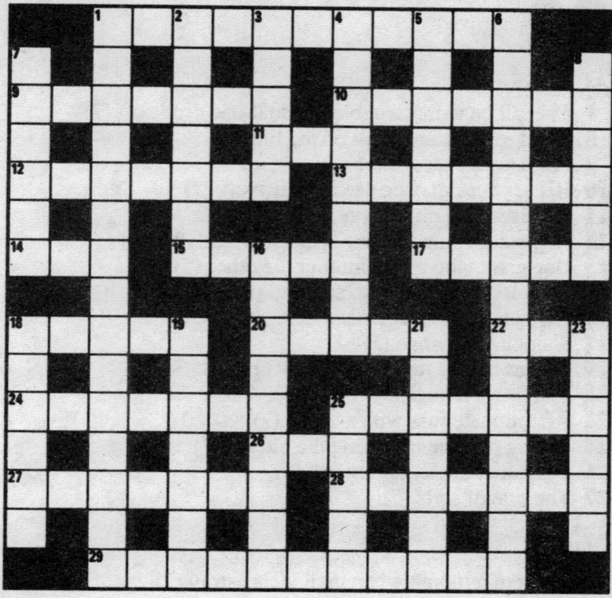

82

ACROSS

1 There'll be worse trouble inside if one drops off (7)
5 Good man taking a call on the line (6)
9 Place to win elsewhere (7)
10 His services may be used exclusively (7)
11 He gives us a bit of a line (3)
12 No protection when one speaks so freely? (11)
13 One giant who might mother the other (5)
14 The girls most likely to succeed (9)
16 Nice place Sean can make here! (9)
17 Shoot a young one (5)
19 Claims before the strains show (11)
22 The firm's lettuce (3)
23 Affectionate fuss with a token (7)
24 Losing no time in putting the bite on (7)
26 Ugly duckling counterpart? (6)
27 The rule of style (7)

DOWN

1 Speak of a month when mail went astray (7)
2 Ritual with the keys? (7, 8)
3 Ready for some games? (3)
4 Move to show irresponsibility (5)
5 Scene of Naval low life (9)
6 Revolution on the course? (5)
7 Pleasant award making very little difference? (4, 11)
8 A form of rot that gets agreement in France (6)
12 Some of your gestures may reveal desire (5)
14 With which one can see what should have happened (9)
15 Moves to provide greater comfort (5)
16 Liked to lose heart in the avenue, maybe (6)
18 Does the cheerful scent of flowers make it? (7)
20 Unsophisticated rising in a Continental resort (5)
21 He's got it! (5)
25 Iron animal? (3)

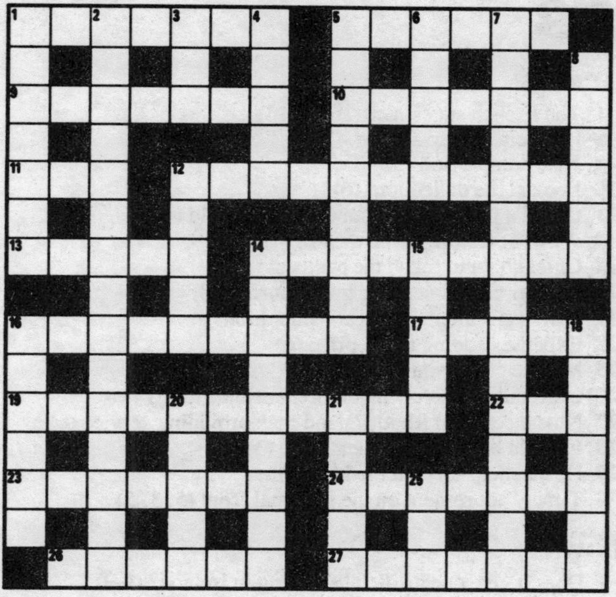
1
2
3
4
5
6
7
8
9
10
11
12
13
14
15
16
17
18
19
20
21
22
23
24
25
26
27

83

ACROSS

1 The French statesman's steak (13)
8 It covers the ground (4)
9 Nice-comparison (3)
10 Look at the deflection! (6)
11 Oaf of a policeman about to shift his hold (10)
13 Way out feature of the theatre (4)
14 Chief about to finish the business (6)
16 Former carrier sending goods abroad (8)
19 Save a girl after riper reconsideration (8)
22 Expenses adding to the price (6)
25 Muscle complaint? (4)
26 Is his talk relatively incomprehensible? (5, 5)
27 Nuisance about Rhode Island man providing service (6)
28 It might be made in a local shop (3)
29 He can help sort out the idea (4)
30 Timely adornment on the personal front (5, 3, 5)

DOWN

1 Does it give one artificial standing in Ireland? (4-3)
2 Leave the foreign gentleman under a prohibition (7)
3 Pose Angie arrived at in the secret service (9)
4 Things come in handy when put to it (3)
5 Jolly chap to signal piracy (5)
6 There's nothing to be gained by this sort of playing! (7)
7 Refuse to go down! (7)
12 Now here is something for you (7)
15 Initially, a sixth sense (3)
17 Looking ahead from the rope pitch (9)
18 Make it a double (3)
20 Its elevation might be a surprise move (7)
21 Think of a light return (7)
23 Able to say good-bye to composition (7)
24 Tank opposed to the Crusader? (7)
26 Put into a depression (5)
28 He's big at Westminster (3)

1
2
3
4
5
6
7
8
9
10
11
12
13
14
15
16
17
18
19
20
21
22
23
24
25
26
27
28
29
30

84

ACROSS

1 No squat Doric rebuilding for the man from Spain (12)
8 Part of St Clement's message (7)
9 It makes one hard-headed (7)
11 He changes out of bedroom rig to appear at the church (10)
12 Face one among the people (4)
14 Does it go to one's head after a day's drinking? (8)
16 Beyond them is forbidden territory (6)
17 My missing mother (3)
19 Sounds like a conversational twist (6)
21 Move the pale disc round (8)
24 We bear the burden of responsibility (4)
25 Funny idea of saucy entertainment? (5, 5)
27 Going with the wind (7)
28 It makes the coat easier to put on (7)
29 Protest about Great War battle coma (12)

DOWN

1 Desire making many mad (7)
2 Not caring to be flung into confusion with the elect (10)
3 Not in the current direction (8)
4 Part of the corset displaced (6)
5 A girl lacking finish, one's sorry to say (4)
6 View all round on the wing (7)
7 Underwear worn by union men? (12)
10 They can be used to clean up the channel (4-8)
13 Pity many take an award with anger! (10)
15 Launching accommodation (3)
18 Skirt disturbing the rest of a statesman (8)
20 Way round to get in as scheduled (7)
22 Hurried in a wild rage to settle matters (7)
23 Makes imitations of iron? (6)
26 It may be laid down to give one standing (4)

1
2
3
4
5
6
7
8
9
10
11
12
13
14
15
16
17
18
19
20
21
22
23
24
25
26
27
28
29

85

ACROSS

6 Global reaction to meeting a friend unexpectedly (3, 1, 5, 5)
9 You do well to do so (6)
10 Chap taking notes with coolness for a living (8)
11 Key passages? (8)
13 Take the air (6)
15 Some sound like dogs as they get on (6)
17 Go ahead and ask for money! (6)
19 Trouble when a top lady loses the way (6)
20 One may not be in time to show this quality (8)
22 Soap acid (8)
24 People about to return help in the middle (6)
26 Brides in no lace may not be worth much (14)

DOWN

1 The new rail advance will be quickly appreciated (4, 5, 5)
2 Bit of a stick-in-the-mud but not without sparkle (4)
3 Turn east with the Navy behind (6)
4 Inclined to attend a Scottish gathering? (8)
5 Beat up some game (4)
7 Morning over wild country can be surprising! (6)
8 Is it read by the man in the pub? (5, 9)
12 One pound shortly to be exchanged for an old coin (5)
14 Take the girl on an aircraft (5)
16 Don't sleep so much if agitated (8)
18 Calm chap's head wrapped in a piece of cloth (6)
21 Man given some bread of sound quality (6)
23 What a blessing there are spectacles inside! (4)
25 Names in another language? (4)

1
2
3
4
5
6
7
8
9
10
11
12
13
14
15
16
17
18
19
20
21
22
23
24
25
26

86

ACROSS

1 Remote part of the hospital for the retarded (8)
5 Figure it might be a famous person (6)
9 Ever ripe to save by reform (8)
10 Charge with bitterness before work (6)
12 Muses as to the number (4)
13 Does it give news of how to wrap the goods in it? (5, 5)
15 Where plant-growing may be learned before five? (7, 6)
19 Long ago when the tale began (4, 4, 1, 4)
23 Having an obstinate ability to hold drink? (10)
25 Qualified to do the can-can, for instance? (4)
28 Quiz game category (6)
29 Guess what it will cost? (8)
30 Looked to see the general blushing (6)
31 Smash and rag about to be explosive? (5-3)

DOWN

1 Going through a dull patch? (6)
2 Covered a bird? (5)
3 A twist of wire may cause a hold-up (4)
4 Back a clergyman to give tongue in Ireland (7)
6 Pedestrian at sea? (5)
7 It enables one to talk rather distantly (9)
8 Way it's done by the man who knows (8)
11 He's in red dyed cloth (4)
14 Having crudely listened to you talking in India? (4)
15 Fruit requiring certain changes at some points (9)
16 Hurry for your money? (3)
17 Cut at a brisk speed (4)
18 A clothing consumer finds it repellent (4-4)
20 Therefore back to a big fellow (4)
21 Inability to recall how men change in the East (7)
22 Go into it to take a break (6)
24 Condemn the overheads (5)
26 It sounds explosive rather than narcotic (5)
27 Express dispproval of escaping steam? (4)

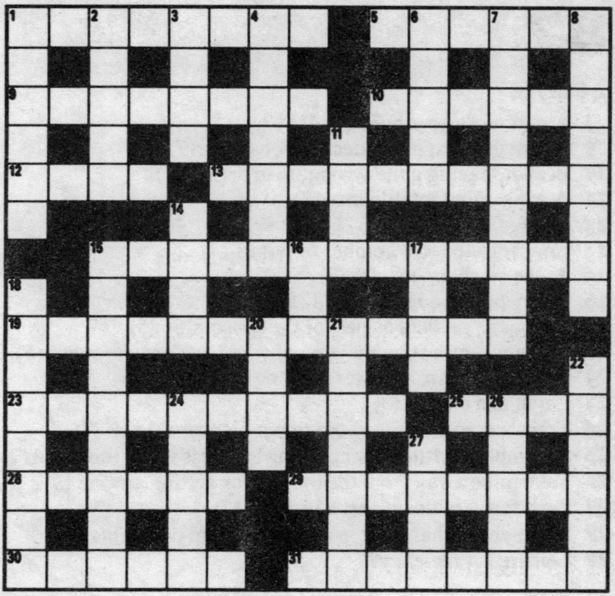
1
2
3
4
5
6
7
8
9
10
11
12
13
14
15
16
17
18
19
20
21
22
23
24
25
26
27
28
29
30
31

87

ACROSS

1 A gunman's goodbye? (7, 4)
9 Polish the image of a decisive crossing (7)
10 Brown, having gone wrong, is in prison (7)
11 A measure of intelligence (3)
12 Lord of the stage (7)
13 Concentrated in a number of points (7)
14 At the same time so far (3)
15 Fancy being in Rita's team! (5)
17 Language garbled as part of the censorship (5)
18 By no means a slow movement when one's in the swim (5)
20 They have their followers among the hounds (5)
22 Catch in a carrier (3)
24 Transfers some idiot about to put his name down (7)
25 Assemble a fortune after starting business with a thousand (7)
26 Take mine away from the the red for getting around (3)
27 Push forward the expert a little bit (7)
28 In which one hasn't been able to keep up payments (7)
29 Leisure for leniency? (4, 2, 5)

DOWN

1 Joy witnessed by everyone in the bus or train? (6, 9)
2 It proves you've had it (7)
3 All but the start of a meal near the centre (5)
4 Only slightly better than a clean quality? (9)
5 A peer's son takes it on in Devon (7)
6 Short-tempered subversives? (3, 5, 7)
7 Nose around the port establishment (6)
8 A tissue might be a sound suggestion for it (6)
16 Getting old enough to be sent round to change the scene (9)
18 Many lights? – heaps! (6)
19 Creature with a pull? (7)
21 Man with a song in ancient Palestine (7)
23 Looking dirty as in an intermediate shade (6)
25 To a point it's daft to change cars (5)

88

ACROSS

1 Like a hero of the boudoir? (7)
5 Fit a record into a holder again (6)
9 Obsolete when used as street clothing? (7)
10 A problem of choice (7)
11 Nothing brought back from Bridlington (3)
12 Oblige to put up (11)
13 Just part of the act (5)
14 Worshipper of all gods who puts a wood god first (9)
16 Quality of that brilliant touch? (9)
17 She may be represented as unarmed (5)
19 Source of a message in tart terms possibly (11)
22 Unidentified person on the way (3)
23 Approve a conclusion reached by devious Rose (7)
24 Cause such surprise as to start undressing (7)
26 He has his orders (6)
27 One of the first to put one in a seaside structure (7)

DOWN

1 Reasons for thinking one's been drinking coffee? (7)
2 He doesn't think big as a patriot (6, 9)
3 Quite a commotion in the dead of night (3)
4 Bucking up with gin? (5)
5 First steps in learning to be offensive? (9)
6 Oil around in the river causing sickness (5)
7 A friend's book or something very like it? (9, 6)
8 It's obvious it gives protection (6)
12 On the look-out for a later move (5)
14 Quiet occupier of the official mansion (9)
15 Hang about as a flier (5)
16 Stretcher for the young? (6)
18 Profligate poet? (7)
20 Fun of a current movement in Berlin (5)
21 One of the more pedestrian vessels? (5)
25 One possible following (3)

1 2 3 4 5 6 7 8 9 10 11 12 13 14 15 16 17 18 19 20 21 22 23 24 25 26 27

89

ACROSS

1 Bernard Shaw character of great richness (13)
8 The layout would be obvious if I were in it (4)
9 Seedy young man? (3)
10 She may be all set to come round (6)
11 Unique skirt brought back before one gets on board (10)
13 Not now where the needle points (4)
14 He has a part in a piece of clever nonsense (6)
16 Release the fifty I scold (8)
19 Score two short (8)
22 Carole's turn to be the wise one (6)
25 Riff-raff at the top? (4)
26 Stopping before starting (10)
27 Go through as a supporter of the church (6)
28 It might be Red or Black (3)
29 Point of prompt payment? (4)
30 Too much the wanton to be carried free? (6, 7)

DOWN

1 Mixture giving me a new angel cake? (7)
2 He works to keep the old lady in clothes (7)
3 One can't do anything to demonstrate it (9)
4 Game for some shut-eye? (3)
5 A number in dispute (5)
6 He may be called on for a put-up job (7)
7 Able to separate five in water (7)
12 Graduate at a point of equilibrium (7)
15 One may cut it in a dance (3)
17 Come back weapon (9)
18 Curve of Parisian triumph (3)
20 Tend not to be on the level (7)
21 Local government official turning up with a man in great form (7)
23 Girl from a different nation (7)
24 Looking likely to roar when a long time in line (7)
26 Push on with the papers? (5)
28 Sorry sound (3)

1 2 3 4 5 6 7
8 9 10
11 12 13
14 15 16 17 18
19 20 21 22 23 24
25 26
27 28 29
30

90

ACROSS

1 Means of giving a hearing to the best performer? (6, 6)
8 Frightened to see Capone with a gun (7)
9 Sudden emergence of rock (7)
11 Disentangles the exact rites somehow (10)
12 Half the directions lead to a motorway (4)
14 Team demonstration of minor entertainment value (4-4)
16 Signals a change of tactic (3-3)
17 Animal back on the road (3)
19 Originator of writing (6)
21 Recording range? (8)
24 Likewise a separate article (4)
25 Working out at last? (10)
27 Concern for the watcher (7)
28 It may have a name for hospitality (3, 4)
29 Blooming good show before lunch! (7-5)

DOWN

1 Performed once more in response (7)
2 Percentage paid for a service appointment? (10)
3 It could spread heat or coolness around (8)
4 Quiet bed-fellow of a bird (6)
5 It's a turn-up for drinkers! (4)
6 Work for a different set without flippancy (7)
7 Teetotaler's pet? (5-7)
10 He did a top job before succeeding (6, 6)
13 Do mini-nude with decreasing effect (10)
15 Fighting fare (3)
18 Note on a drink feature from which we can learn (8)
20 Sound of uncertainty (7)
22 Three in college (7)
23 No good to rent possibly (6)
26 Damaged as far as the Navy is concerned (4)

1
2
3
4
5
6
7
8
9
10
11
12
13
14
15
16
17
18
19
20
21
22
23
24
25
26
27
28
29

91

ACROSS

6 Award for coming clean? (5, 2, 3, 4)
9 Cunning plan for sound breathing? (6)
10 Bird taking a late glass of beer? (8)
11 Groan weirdly and expire in something diaphanous (8)
13 Pass a one-way error (6)
15 Moral improvement (6)
17 The place for a rabbit (6)
19 He's the third! (6)
20 Not a member of the present assembly (8)
22 Heavenly subject for the doctor (8)
24 Place to work away from the rink (6)
26 Pause when there's room for a further intake (9-5)

DOWN

1 A better parent than those with actual children? (6, 8)
2 Provides more of a tool, one might say (4)
3 One day he'll finish being a mate (6)
4 Substance almost making a ruler envious (8)
5 Border on an objection (4)
7 On hand to make a point, perhaps (6)
8 One can see through their colourful representations (14)
12 A last turn to show how the land lies (5)
14 It has major growth potential (5)
16 Torch carried by an admirer over the door? (8)
18 Don't allow any inside the tree (6)
21 Liverpudlian science on the river (6)
23 One didn't linger in the Middle East (4)
25 Racing pad? (4)

92

ACROSS

1 Buying the means of exerting force (8)
5 I leave the returning mini vehicle in a cloud (6)
9 Classical front triangle (8)
10 One cad might become a church officer (6)
12 Refusal to be on time (4)
13 It helps the insider to get some air (10)
15 Rum seat for a Rugby team? (4, 4, 5)
19 Haystack builders value in Hertfordshire (13)
23 One of small intellect to look after the young? (4-6)
25 Not the best people at the top (4)
28 Clever enough to see if any rib is broken (6)
29 Give the army craftsmen an indicator for putting right (8)
30 Points to a rude change that will last (6)
31 For playing David's works? (8)

DOWN

1 Laying on some music? (6)
2 Communication this time in port (5)
3 The man takes a politician to supply the dope (4)
4 Bus name seen in a different light (7)
6 One transaction is perfect! (5)
7 Fed-up limits (4, 5)
8 It's on Roy to provide the resonance (8)
11 Silence with a rising retort (4)
14 Fighting keeps many in lively condition (4)
15 Laid-down basis for keeping out of the mire (4)
16 Unwise character of Bray? (3)
17 Bottle-neck city? (4)
18 Likely to be in the running (8)
20 Days of wonder (4)
21 In view of the fact that this place was surrounded (7)
22 Possibly inviting sniffy disapproval (6)
24 Person of low extraction (5)
26 Many exist like the man of India (5)
27 Avenging Emma? (4)

1
2
3
4
5
6
7
8
9
10
11
12
13
14
15
16
17
18
19
20
21
22
23
24
25
26
27
28
29
30
31

93

ACROSS

1 He's marvellously crazy! (7, 4)
9 Many a disturbance can cause injury (7)
10 Convince the recipient that he's had enough? (7)
11 Ignore a possible reduction? (3)
12 Beg to mend the net tear (7)
13 Possible venue for a down-to-earth experience (7)
14 Note the carrier's return (3)
15 Quite a number of notes (5)
17 It gives a clearer outlook (5)
18 Wood god who may stray around (5)
20 Yet another edition, what's more! (5)
22 Grave comment on a tearaway? (3)
24 Reverses the turn with relaxing effect (7)
25 Tell the story of the close election (7)
26 Not quite a versifier though he did write some (3)
27 Island favouring the Amos reform (7)
28 A rebellion coming up (7)
29 Cash one might not live to collect (6, 5)

DOWN

1 Have fun spreading communist propaganda? (5, 3, 4, 3)
2 Push again to keep down (7)
3 Standing before the court briefly (5)
4 Some of the Bible mates upset in part of a camp (9)
5 Get too big for what you've got on (7)
6 Missed bus, for example (4, 11)
7 A lot written by way of stating what one believes (6)
8 It might be open for Pearl to be discovered (6)
16 Area where no coverage is provided (4, 5)
18 Too pompous to have a window open? (6)
19 Hurry over business with the Navy in town (7)
21 Running one may be a put-up job (7)
23 Soup for the drug era? (6)
25 Land of the genuine monkey's head (5)

94

ACROSS

1 Where one may hear the sound of cattle? (7)
5 Sing when there's a fight and you start bleeding (6)
9 Sound electrifying (7)
10 The girl looks different having lost weight (7)
11 Enough to express disgust when one's backed away (3)
12 One of ten to obey (11)
13 Strange way to reach the lake (5)
14 The man in the chair (9)
16 Where they keep wine for sale? (9)
17 People go to court to make them plain (5)
19 Something's going to happen, it's felt (11)
22 Take nothing from an old airship in port (3)
23 Understand how to cash in (7)
24 Incline to the German swimmer (7)
26 One way to mend a tester (6)
27 Given the business with generosity (7)

DOWN

1 It's delivery can be instructive (7)
2 Further outlook usually uncertain (7, 8)
3 Vessel for saving (3)
4 It's all in the mind (5)
5 Pedestrian exercise in royal matiness (9)
6 Showed displeasure at a new grade (5)
7 They entitle the traveller to corresponding advances (7, 2, 6)
8 Depression caused by a bombing attack? (6)
12 See if it's right to have all those squares? (5)
14 Outstanding men in port reorganisation (9)
15 Having been sent down (5)
16 Wonderful Balkan character getting up inside (6)
18 Searched to get rid of dirt (7)
20 Nothing animated for her! (5)
21 The detached property has found a tenant (5)
25 Time to get through half the business (3)

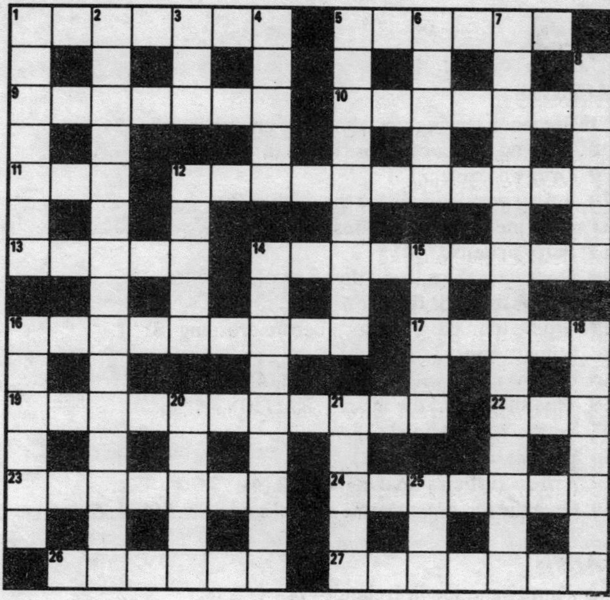
1
2
3
4
5
6
7
8
9
10
11
12
13
14
15
16
17
18
19
20
21
22
23
24
25
26
27

95

ACROSS

1 Someone teasing you about the church here? (13)
8 Take no notice of a nose being turned up (4)
9 Drug container? (3)
10 It may provide digs for the soldier (6)
11 How the clergyman cares! (10)
13 Party in defeat? (4)
14 Does it teach us to cut down on clothes? (6)
16 This is the end! (8)
19 Where to make a fast turn before crossing (8)
22 Sting to anger? (6)
25 Preseverance gets her included (4)
26 This should put the matter right (10)
27 Person of standing? (6)
28 Subject of the queen (3)
29 Artless ruffian's final comeback (4)
30 Give the ice-cream some disciplined form? (4, 4, 5)

DOWN

1 Family auction in Ireland? (7)
2 Discusses a girl with a set-up (7)
3 Talk of international contact (9)
4 Basis of a standing rebuke (3)
5 Smart enough not to agree about a race (5)
6 One might be asked to prove it (7)
7 He's in the Service now (7)
12 Wash the French below (7)
15 Spring in Belgium (3)
17 That wound-up feeling (9)
18 Back in the Navy (3)
20 It's hard to cover a foot extension (3-4)
21 Desperate to put it up in foreign currency (7)
23 A Titian dream fairy (7)
24 Distinguished-looking man in the Orient (7)
26 Dog of a royal favourite (5)
28 It may hang before flight (3)

96

ACROSS

1 Story in revealing pictures? (5, 7)
8 Transport to inflation? (7)
9 After this let change be a symbol! (7)
11 Mate in the cast? (10)
12 Worry about a decoration? (4)
14 It makes saving less boring (8)
16 At one's best, you can tell (6)
17 Made a cutting observation? (3)
19 Took too much of the animal? (6)
21 Arrangement for which one might get backing (8)
24 Give offence with a piece of sacrilege (4)
25 Encouraging one to be a consumer (10)
27 One's place in life when one has arrived? (7)
28 Zero distances for shooting fruit (7)
29 Town and country seat (12)

DOWN

1 Domestic rest disturbed when a vehicle comes in (7)
2 Check made necessary by the arrival of more troops (10)
3 Best to have abolished the House of Lords? (8)
4 Getting something done, one takes it (6)
5 Lean, joining the king in meditation (4)
6 Ration distribution adding nothing in Canada (7)
7 Richard shops around for instruments (12)
10 There are small creatures in his study (12)
13 Too coarse to be a singer's lass? (10)
15 Is a new art from his craft? (3)
18 We pick a bloom up and become beastly! (8)
20 He got stoned in a big way (7)
22 Old Bob covered when he drank (7)
23 Absorbing way to clean up (6)
26 Yearn for an absent girl? (4)

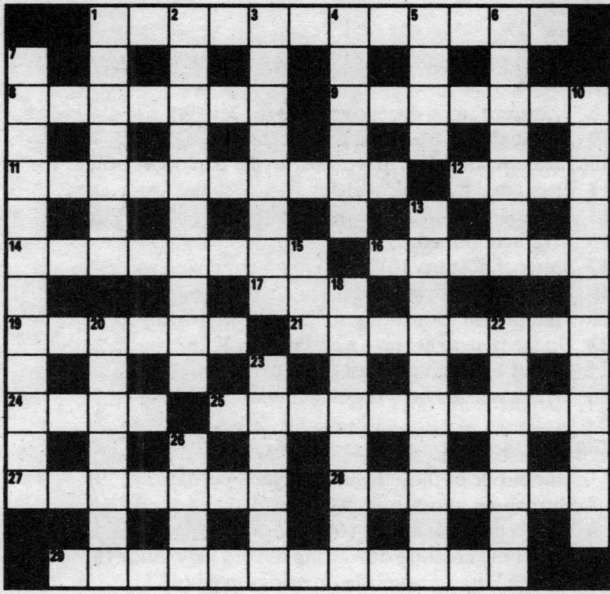
1
2
3
4
5
6
7
8
9
10
11
12
13
14
15
16
17
18
19
20
21
22
23
24
25
26
27
28
29

97

ACROSS

6 Transporting in deceptive style (6, 3, 1, 4)
9 Horrified at a fractured gas hat (6)
10 Pleasant sort of chap working in the personnel office? (8)
11 Frustrated by drink? (8)
13 Style of a girl in a male address (6)
15 Live in dignified style (6)
17 Spirit of hostility (6)
19 Puts off out of respect? (6)
20 Plump limb for making such a delivery (5-3)
22 Up the pole to achieve a certain level? (8)
24 Regret a morning in fast time (6)
26 What's needed here is quick thinking (8, 2, 4)

DOWN

1 Star of one of those Jesus musicals, perhaps? (5, 9)
2 Bird going into a joint, we hear (4)
3 Take a bit from a song (6)
4 Fearsome creature devouring the old lady guide (8)
5 What a bore transvestite dressing-up is! (4)
7 Right away from our companions we can be devils! (6)
8 Song brayed to the balcony? (6, 8)
12 East end teas mixed according to one's liking (5)
14 Identified me in Dan's rising (5)
16 Scorns what may be said badly in rows (8)
18 Game between banks? (6)
21 Support in rising (6)
23 It may have an instinctive following (4)
25 Most important source of water (4)

98

ACROSS

1 Concert artist's superior standing (8)
5 Personal cover for the final goïng-away (6)
9 Prospect of a TV show (8)
10 Getting into deep water (6)
12 Otherwise taken from a modern novel sequence (4)
13 Unable to endure a non-litter arrangement (10)
15 Insist on a decision when violence is in question (5, 3, 5)
19 It provides energy along certain lines (7, 6)
23 He lives in the place wearing the garment of a worker (10)
25 Rousing send-off? (4)
28 Provide what you can pay (6)
29 Old Rover could be a top person (8)
30 Afraid to be colourful? (6)
31 Did he express surprise in his art? (8)

DOWN

1 With corn it amounts to a very little rent (6)
2 She's in the champagne set (5)
3 The way things are done in class (4)
4 Story of a love affair (7)
6 Nothing directly transmitted by that drab girl (5)
7 Eric's safe to come round for something to eat (9)
8 Near the adornments worn in retirement (8)
11 Ring up Winnie (4)
14 The short haircut gang (4)
15 Bad enough to cause fear (9)
16 Drive away from here (3)
17 Rainbow flower (4)
18 The usual charge for arms? (8)
20 On the other hand one will identify the snowman (4)
21 City absorbing some of the vehicles after a time (7)
22 Front man with a following (6)
24 Trade unionist around the old place looking an ass (5)
26 A payment to be made in the island (5)
27 In which one may be up when angry (4)

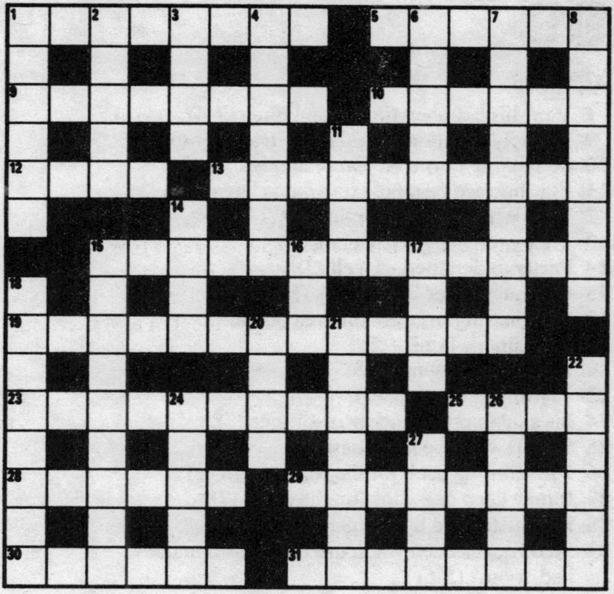
1
2
3
4
5
6
7
8
9
10
11
12
13
14
15
16
17
18
19
20
21
22
23
24
25
26
27
28
29
30
31

99

ACROSS

1 Very little money for rearing birds (7-4)
9 Possibly inflationary aid to the traveller (3, 4)
10 Something burned to cause annoyance (7)
11 For instance take note of what is laid down (3)
12 Tells where the connection is (7)
13 They promote good feeling (7)
14 Partly understood as well (3)
15 Capital manner in business (5)
17 Start putting trousers on in Scotland (5)
18 Godfather's family (5)
20 Place for the winner (5)
22 Try to acquire taste (3)
24 It's said to reject both possibilities (7)
25 So sure I can be in earnest! (7)
26 I am coming back for the foreign girl (3)
27 It may keep one afloat on the canal (7)
28 He's distressed by a departure (7)
29 Stabiliser needed when there's a storm in the bed-room? (5-6)

DOWN

1 People one knows as all-rounders? (6, 2, 7)
2 Like the traditional silly villager (7)
3 Supporters of the devout (5)
4 The hour being altered, he's easily contacted (9)
5 Ways to sing that charm (7)
6 One may find trouble doing a turn here (9, 6)
7 Motoring nonsense provides some incentive (6)
8 Motive for using the mind? (6)
16 His assistance to the police can be telling (9)
18 Chap with time to cope (6)
19 Convert the loan for a place in Ireland (7)
21 Connected after a lot of tunnelling? (7)
23 Fool turning up to attempt some baking (6)
25 The simple saint (5)

1
2
3
4
5
6
7
8
9
10
11
12
13
14
15
16
17
18
19
20
21
22
23
24
25
26
27
28
29

100

ACROSS

1 There should be some pickings here (7)
5 Rose can figure the pattern (6)
9 Having some noted felicities (7)
10 Tar on a tree in Cornwall (7)
11 Drum cover (3)
12 Hide the top man in Surrey (11)
13 Act crudely when there's this trouble with the barn (5)
14 Wrong one in the sourer mixture (9)
16 Number a few for a reel (9)
17 Place of judgment? (5)
19 Almost in an efficient way (11)
22 Due to being pronounced poetry (3)
23 It all started with these (7)
24 After the explosion the picture may be enlarged (5, 2)
26 It can be lowered in a winking! (6)
27 Every one agreed to be reduced (7)

DOWN

1 Ways to escape (7)
2 Where the body exerts weight is no laughing matter! (6, 2, 7)
3 He'd be great if he put on colour! (3)
4 Wing in the mouth (5)
5 Unload and fire (9)
6 Grinder at the back (5)
7 He attended the opening after the show closed (5-4, 6)
8 One part of hell where it's dark (6)
12 That's as far as you can go (5)
14 Got devil out of it! (9)
15 Quick enough to get a bite or two? (5)
16 Use to smash my pole (6)
18 Very much inclined to be soaked? (7)
20 That's going to be the material! (5)
21 Upset by Ali in North Africa (5)
25 No light lover (3)

1
2
3
4
5
6
7
8
9
10
11
12
13
14
15
16
17
18
19
20
21
22
23
24
25
26
27

101

ACROSS

1 Old-fashioned blonde? You've hit it exactly! (4, 3, 6)
8 Size of a real room (4)
9 Girl turning back for a sparkler (3)
10 Part of the foot that keeps the rhythm (6)
11 Moves uncertainly out of a villa sect (10)
13 Money memo? (4)
14 It's morning and a girl appears (6)
16 They don't make themselves clear (8)
19 Noisy description of a designer? (8)
22 Can't give a girl a blessed start (6)
25 Catch on to a small branch? (4)
26 This should put the matter right (10)
27 He gives a service (6)
28 Keep out the lawyers (3)
29 Point on which one might pay cash (4)
30 Hydrant for holiday-makers? (8-5)

DOWN

1 Prepare to fight below the elbow (7)
2 Spike comes up after I give thanks as a foreigner (7)
3 Is it served at the harpists' tea? (5-4)
4 Hold-up taking a crazy turn (3)
5 Double alternative (5)
6 Powerful shooting capacity is expected from this side (7)
7 Oriental clergyman in a constructive role (7)
12 Met up with pert twister who leads one astray (7)
15 She's the same either way (3)
17 Present day drama? Cheese it! (9)
18 Go out and make a beach exposure (3)
20 No intellectual with a lot of hair in front? (3-4)
21 Nothing is done to show it (7)
23 Aerial worker bringing up a girl (7)
24 Looking like a royal beast (7)
26 Provide an animal with a royal device (5)
28 What a blessing he is on! (3)

1 2 3 4 5 6 7
8 9 10
11 12 13
14 15 16 17 18
19 20 21 22 23 24
25 26
27 28 29
30

102

ACROSS

1 Not so many people about after this (12)
8 Unsuccessful competitor in a hurry too (4-3)
9 Admitted the old lady had a man with her (7)
11 Thin grains possibly having a dull effect (10)
12 Give me some nuts if that's what's on offer (4)
14 Man from the East giving Hull a bad turn (8)
16 Spirit of progress on the road (6)
17 It's supplied in some volume in the main (3)
19 It's seen not to be real (6)
21 Taking abrasive action when getting together (8)
24 You may be left with it after tearing off (4)
25 Fur failing to keep one feature warm, it's said (10)
27 Bad man with a parent taking one in metal (7)
28 Pay for fractured emu ribs (7)
29 Real pal when wanted, poor chap? (6, 2, 4)

DOWN

1 Wanted to turn the side over to colour (7)
2 Peer is disturbed about Union Jack mockery (10)
3 Drink container offering striking practice (5-3)
4 Supporter at last giving the story (6)
5 Bait put up to catch one (4)
6 Not a house coat that one will keep no longer? (7)
7 Noted assembly on the march (7, 5)
10 More than usually expressionless in a protected light (6-6)
13 Could be taken off a chalet bed, perhaps (10)
15 Possesses the means of expressing amusement? (3)
18 Metre reading (8)
20 Seeming more plump (7)
22 Crooked Bill is obviously not top drawer (3-4)
23 He's mad at being so humiliated! (6)
26 The digger's claim? (4)

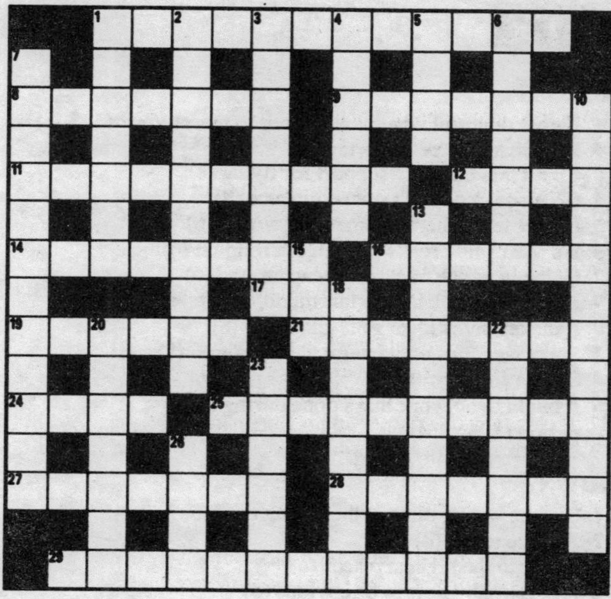
1
2
3
4
5
6
7
8
9
10
11
12
13
14
15
16
17
18
19
20
21
22
23
24
25
26
27
28
29

103

ACROSS

6 Father doubtful when you ask her to marry you? (3, 3, 8)
9 Stuff that may be important (6)
10 First-class Catholic support for flying (8)
11 Go up on Scotland's own eminence (8)
13 Desert when there's something wrong (6)
15 It's Mao who breaks up Chinese religion (6)
17 Game in which one has to leap around (6)
19 Bill comes back after a fair muddle overseas (6)
20 It makes investment so fascinating! (8)
22 Sinks warships on a fateful day in March (8)
24 She's a survivor (6)
26 It ought to be work that's done during this period (2, 3, 5, 4)

DOWN

1 Say the wrong thing at the wrong time (5, 3, 2, 4)
2 A place to see (4)
3 Guide to the highest places (6)
4 Ask Barnaby how to be envious (8)
5 Quite a commotion in the kitchen? (4)
7 Starting quietly and isn't commonly odd (6)
8 It may be revealed as a breach of the law (8, 6)
12 She pulls a boy up about honour (5)
14 Knock down to a low domestic level (5)
16 Half of some sporting aloofness (5-3)
18 Affectionately vulgar reference to the mouth? (6)
21 Bird disease? (6)
23 This way home dropping me off in London (4)
25 Deposited fifty with some assistance (4)

104

ACROSS

1 Means of a hold-up at the opening (8)
5 Where Mother's baby sleeps, lucky thing! (6)
9 Likely to fall with too much weight spinning? (3-5)
10 Commemorative meal? (6)
12 Do some scratch work as an artist? (4)
13 Not planned in relation to what's happening? (10)
15 Taken unawares as a racing tipster? (6, 7)
19 They don't quite add up when it's Princess Decia's turn (13)
23 Means of sending some vegetables by tube (10)
25 Judge the bad man before one (4)
28 Ladies reform their aspirations (6)
29 Compact biscuit (8)
30 Old king of the tenors (6)
31 Moved to a higher position (8)

DOWN

1 Understand how to pick (6)
2 It may be talked about (5)
3 The hunting man as outsider? (4)
4 Not the first to try to keep quiet about what happened (7)
6 In mine she'd be a different girl! (5)
7 Beastly extensions to a garment (4-5)
8 Express disapproval when the eagle strays from protection (8)
11 Wild celebrity (4)
14 Country talk when the phone rings (4)
15 Do they enable one to click as an entertainer? (9)
16 Eastern import going to pot (3)
17 A cause of ill-feeling? (4)
18 It makes one a member of the family (8)
20 Scheme to get some land (4)
21 Riles in pointed fashion? (7)
22 Bad to be provided with something to burn? (6)
24 He will provide nothing by way of greeting (5)
26 Prize for a protégée (5)
27 Perhaps eastern churches have it inside (4)

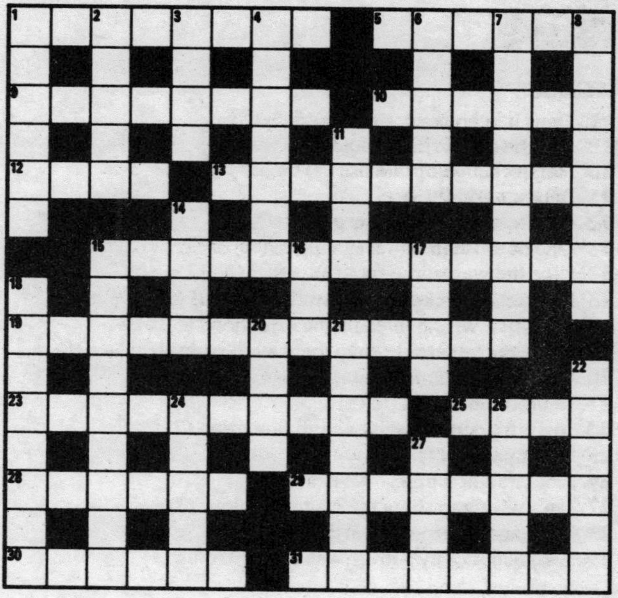
1 2 3 4 5 6 7 8 9 10 11 12 13 14 15 16 17 18 19 20 21 22 23 24 25 26 27 28 29 30 31

105

ACROSS

1 Does it keep crazy time? (6-5)
9 Not the sky-writing route (7)
10 Harsh change of rate use (7)
11 Baba's so odd! (3)
12 Old Rose may be a new girl (7)
13 One of those things that happen (7)
14 Like the way of the fool (3)
15 It could be sticky if the gems aren't real! (5)
17 Anything wrong in enduring affection? (5)
18 Show the venerable chap the way to sprinkle water (5)
20 Order of poetic feet (5)
22 Revolutionary centre (3)
24 Just a bit depressed by an inflammation (7)
25 Trendy ball? (7)
26 Not straight whisky, we hear (3)
27 Ian's wrong to show the route in colour (7)
28 Turn again before the artist falls (7)
29 Lady Chatterley's lover was one of them (11)

DOWN

1 Result of taking a crash course? (8, 7)
2 Sound like a bird urging on a horse (7)
3 Surplus batches of deliveries? (5)
4 Creature of colourful adaptability (9)
5 Got us in, perhaps, by causing displacement (7)
6 Sign of uninviting greenery (4, 3, 3, 5)
7 Desert the Gunners for a girl (6)
8 Hard to see the clergyman coming up inside (6)
16 It induces that sinking feeling (9)
18 Old soldier finding the wrong woman at the Bull's Head (6)
19 He's sweet in the garden (7)
21 Conditions in which mail, etc., is distributed (7)
23 He has a job to provide drink (6)
25 Reason for feeling? (5)

1
2
3
4
5
6
7
8
9
10
11
12
13
14
15
16
17
18
19
20
21
22
23
24
25
26
27
28
29

106

ACROSS

1 Pie accessory on stage (7)
5 Take up the problem in a rough sea (6)
9 Train me somehow to arrange cover (7)
10 Some of the Scots have a desire to punish (7)
11 It colours one's communication (3)
12 Giving orders to learn? (11)
13 The big match at last! (5)
14 Study the offer of a competitor (9)
16 Knowledge required to emerge from the peer's exit (9)
17 One isn't sure if one's in it (5)
19 Solicitation corresponding to slavery? (5-6)
22 The blame's on the man who takes it (3)
23 All-round build-up (7)
24 Here is something you needn't pay for! (7)
26 Where being on the outside has its benefits? (6)
27 Wooden attendant? (7)

DOWN

1 Quite a character if rather loud for the city (7)
2 It covers the cut (8-7)
3 Time to follow a bird in Dorset (3)
4 Fruit for occasions (5)
5 Promise of security (9)
6 He's not the excitable sort (5)
7 Service flat, for instance? (7, 8)
8 Fast-moving transfer to REME (6)
12 He'll do nothing if badly riled (5)
14 Illegal gesture subversive of law and order? (5, 4)
15 Churchman reading the article in Spanish and German (5)
16 He's with you all the way (6)
18 He may provide an opening for drinkers (7)
20 Not quite time to take on material (5)
21 Given similar parts when the script is prepared? (5)
25 She's another girl when embracing wild Dan (3)

107

ACROSS

1 The blooming delight of being on the move? (10, 3)
8 Lovely girl to provide something to eat! (4)
9 Old Egypt's fatal biter (3)
10 Ask a person to depart (6)
11 He moves differently from train speed (10)
13 Right to divert a great river (4)
14 Tommy strikes a very hard note (6)
16 Strain of fast driving to see the other woman (8)
19 News of the missile getting in (8)
22 So hard to be mocking? (6)
25 Go away, Lady, you're a singer! (4)
26 Soft-centre lover (10)
27 He's No. 1 at the finish (6)
28 Bird of the Lowlands (3)
29 Arthur initially hurried off the Irish Coast (4)
30 Spots of Teuton contact? (6, 7)

DOWN

1 Aircraft in which I would be in the river (7)
2 He's quick to put the tale around (7)
3 Tan cement mixed according to law (9)
4 It may be given as cheek (3)
5 Does he hold an at-home for thieves? (5)
6 He keeps things moving in the air (7)
7 They're well known for their doodles (7)
12 Big chaps in semi-confusion (7)
15 General rising in the water (3)
17 Just a spot of light (9)
18 One makes a change in time (3)
20 Getting the Nations together at Lake Success? (7)
21 A letter notifies his driving status (7)
23 Complete coverage for the worker (7)
24 Are they made with no provision for subsequent retreat? (7)
26 Ray is around in the Middle East (5)
28 A measure of resistance (3)

108

ACROSS

1 Italy covered in very pretty style (12)
8 Has a vehicle inside for the cigars (7)
9 Permit for wildness? (7)
11 Miles astray with a ringing noise that's deceptive (10)
12 He has a beer before the calls start (4)
14 On yacht, perhaps, being rude (8)
16 For her to get a gun is a bit daft! (6)
17 Object of a summit revolution! (3)
19 They give sheer satisfaction (6)
21 Does one know when it's time to bark? (5-3)
24 Big embrace given by direction (4)
25 Neither a Yankee nor a Yorkshireman (10)
27 Man to throw a piece of earthenware (7)
28 Is he a fair-weather friend? (7)
29 In which we may learn how to take leave? (6, 6)

DOWN

1 Thinks of the way one makes a bequest (7)
2 Hiding many on an occasion with a fish (10)
3 Torn about the team living here (8)
4 It figures in a story the New Testament provides (6)
5 It's bad when one isn't quite top man (4)
6 No all-in contortions to make one fat (7)
7 Best craft in the contest! (12)
10 It may decide what you get for your money in Europe (8, 4)
13 They go in for runs (10)
15 Drag to where the wickedness starts (3)
18 This place could be in someone else's style (8)
20 Not one of the big-tonnage vessels (7)
22 Little George Dunn thrown into prison (7)
23 Regent's Georgian number (6)
26 Keep it up for good cheer (4)

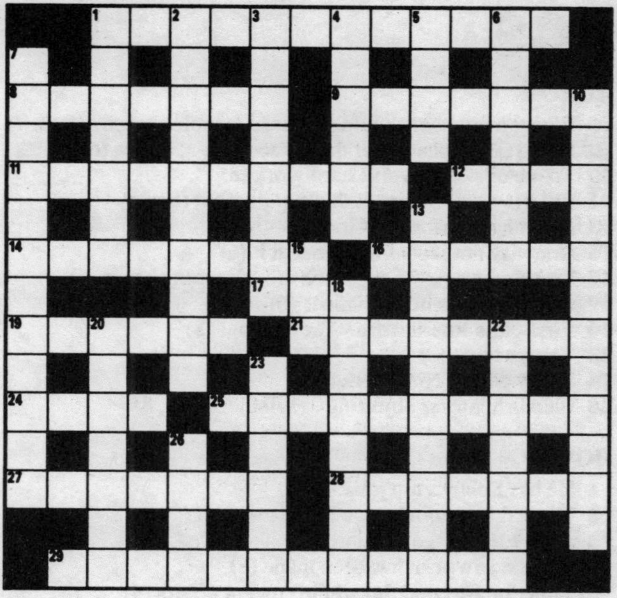
1 2 3 4 5 6 7 8 9 10 11 12 13 14 15 16 17 18 19 20 21 22 23 24 25 26 27 28 29

109

ACROSS

6 Where a member should not make a noble speech? (5, 2, 7)
9 Count taking the last of the Saracens to America (6)
10 To me oils can involve hard work (8)
11 Bill has been ordained, that's quite right (8)
13 Meaning to bring stuff in (6)
15 One may not see what's beneath it (6)
17 Brave of the girl to approach the officer in charge (6)
19 Gain gratitude in a container (6)
20 First-class Russian drink for the dog! (8)
22 Terrier town (8)
24 Shady part of New York (6)
26 Fiendish lawyer objecting to sainthood? (6, 8)

DOWN

1 He has Bobby's top job (5, 9)
2 There'll be a commotion if one makes it (4)
3 Aspire to change a country (6)
4 Quite sure a print has been made (8)
5 Time for a second thought in current affairs (4)
7 Cause to get fed up (6)
8 Two follows on in it (9, 5)
12 Last month the artist was even more so! (5)
14 How a lion feels about its young? (5)
16 Study poetry so as to be able to talk (8)
18 Saddened to see Father knocking Enid about (6)
21 It enables the award winner to present a colourful front (6)
23 Change of air on the way causing bad weather (4)
25 Put on in the river (4)

110

ACROSS

1 Chap to train a monkey (8)
5 Great spinner providing entertainment (3, 3)
9 Brief job notification? (8)
10 Where to get a cool drink at work (6)
12 Land in Paisley without wages (4)
13 Dramatist to portray an early aviator (10)
15 Europeans, it seems, they have a close relationship (7-6)
19 It's not very likely! (13)
23 Wildly excited act in Corby (10)
25 Indication of past pain (4)
28 Run and get changed in a hurry (6)
29 Chap at a party getting nothing back for music (8)
30 Just a little whisper (6)
31 Inclinations to adopt the Pisan style? (8)

DOWN

1 Chart most of the line of sands (6)
2 Sounding like the hooter (5)
3 It's torture to do a stretch on it! (4)
4 Rock singer (7)
6 Deduce finer change (5)
7 Slender and sticky like the what's-its-name (9)
8 Tip angle the other way when folding (8)
11 They have it in a successful resolution (4)
14 Game to act at Lulu's end (4)
15 Transcribe without error if it allows you to (9)
16 Catch a familiar politician (3)
17 The way to become an outsider (4)
18 Attach less importance to the price cut (8)
20 Bob's sister? (4)
21 Copy one on the road to the gallery (7)
22 Marks with burning wood? (6)
24 Commonplace girl turning up at the Bull's Head (5)
26 He has the business when nothing arises (5)
27 All-round noise provided by a god (4)

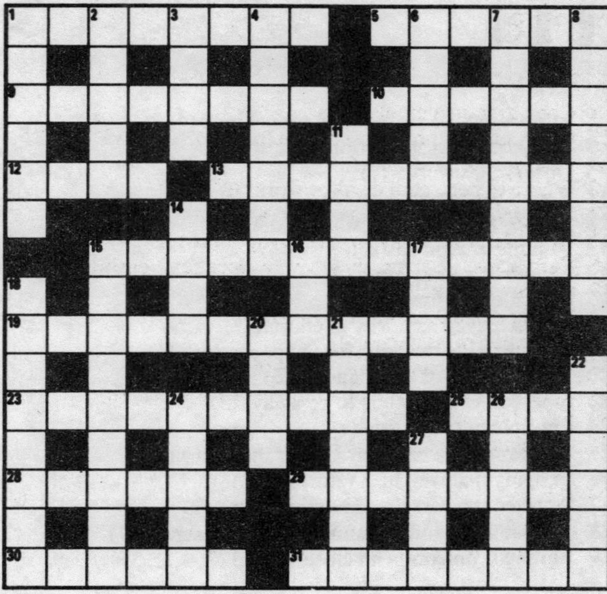
1 2 3 4 5 6 7 8
9 10
11
12 13
14
15 16 17
18
19 20 21
22
23 24 25 26
27
28 29
30 31

111

ACROSS

1 In a position to run without crouching? (4, 7)
9 Talk about dissatisfaction! (7)
10 Observe it's wordy (7)
11 Regret the French way (3)
12 Abuses for reforming sin and lust (7)
13 Resumé of road casualties? (3-4)
14 Length of yellow cloth (3)
15 Pale after the fire? (5)
17 He's achieved seniority in church (5)
18 They provide the basis for the paperwork (5)
20 One works hard to produce it (5)
22 A person you may beg to go away! (3)
24 Rig Lola out as an ape (7)
25 A little science can turn a cheer into a cry (7)
26 Denying that weight is returning (3)
27 Rejected the vessel and hurried round (7)
28 A horse and another animal in literal disarray (7)
29 Agree to confront with close vision! (3, 3, 2, 3)

DOWN

1 Beginnings of growth in EEC control of farm produce? (8, 7)
2 Oil able to be refined in plant (7)
3 They make things work (5)
4 High respect for the Irishman's priest (9)
5 One rang the changes in the river (7)
6 Unbelievably saintly? (3, 4, 2, 2, 4)
7 I get in to make a fiery start (6)
8 Note how to enter the North another way (6)
16 Farming for men only? (9)
18 Take in a condensed version (6)
19 Keep it without saying a word (7)
21 Houses from which one can view the game? (7)
23 Dig up from a historian (6)
25 Begin to show alarm (5)

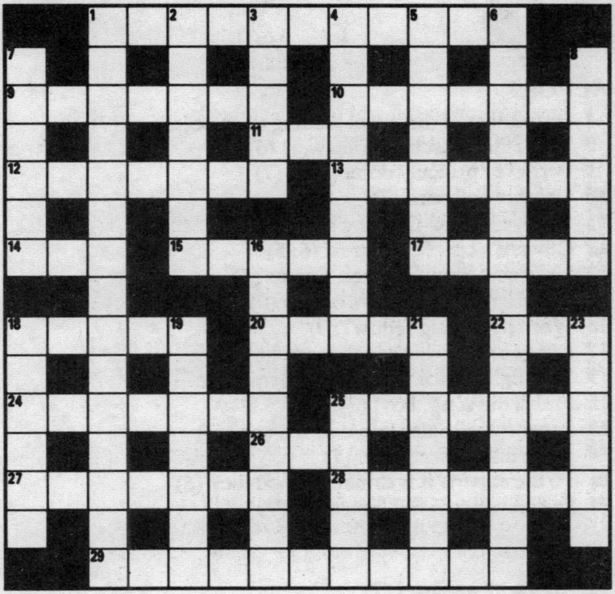
1
2
3
4
5
6
7
8
9
10
11
12
13
14
15
16
17
18
19
20
21
22
23
24
25
26
27
28
29

112

ACROSS

1 Instrument of dismissal leading to an objection (7)
5 Why, this must be the answer! (6)
9 Period of princely dominance (7)
10 Colours on board (7)
11 The well-know G-string manner? (3)
12 Coward's tasteful contrast (6, 5)
13 Let it somehow be given a name (5)
14 Make a note of doctor's orders (9)
16 Worn by the big fellow? (9)
17 Longs to see what's in the tea-chest (5)
19 Too high a price front being permissive? (11)
22 Finish the song, boy! (3)
23 Support the replacement of red ones (7)
24 A devilish description! (7)
26 To the experts it is drinkers' good luck (6)
27 Sex and dope tie-up revealed! (7)

DOWN

1 Man with a master (7)
2 It keeps the smoker away from tobacco (9-6)
3 Edible hair-do (3)
4 Meeting to test a good man (5)
5 Be there instead to put in the picture (9)
6 Mountains of maps (5)
7 Like a properly directed train (2, 3, 5, 5)
8 Proverbial recipient of black abuse (6)
12 Sound sheepish when the table is overturned (5)
14 Well-known men in port to turn round (9)
15 Follow one out of the carriage (5)
16 Go quietly with the girl, little beast! (6)
18 Wrongly deduce that one is led astray (7)
20 His chair is on the mountain (5)
21 Send out the children (5)
25 Advice on what to give? (3)

1
2
3
4
5
6
7
8
9
10
11
12
13
14
15
16
17
18
19
20
21
22
23
24
25
26
27

113

ACROSS

1 Does it enable noise to be kept down for library work? (6, 7)
8 Go west at the Nag's Head for cover (4)
9 Holder of the ashes (3)
10 I leave the train before religion brings on a coma (6)
11 The dull fig can be very pleasant (10)
13 Club for smoother folk? (4)
14 Mark the way a soldier returns with Mother (6)
16 Extend Noel's turn on the way in (8)
19 Outlines some revue items (8)
22 Former displaced temp given immunity (6)
25 Shape for the usual procedure (4)
26 Secret? But it's an advertisement! (10)
27 Tea permitted in the home (6)
28 Not a cat to copy! (3)
29 Musical part of money? (4)
30 What is expected at the bonfire party? (4, 9)

DOWN

1 Not evil perhaps, just rough (7)
2 Arriving between flights (7)
3 Contribution to cleaner speech? (5-4)
4 Able to be repeated in a dance (3)
5 Two boys in South Africa (5)
6 Intake town? (7)
7 Exclusive idea of the disputing boss (7)
12 No charge is put up on a flower (7)
15 Fish quietly removed for him (3)
17 Occupy the top bunk too long? (9)
18 Reason for a hole in the pullover (3)
20 What you need for a skilled performance (4-3)
21 Does it hold water in the lock? (7)
23 Find fee made over to old Turk (7)
24 Said to have hurried forward into town (7)
26 Many tear about to provide food (5)
28 Car crash round the bend (3)

114

ACROSS

1 Half the roundhouse looks like this! (12)
8 What many think when it's public (7)
9 The craft of the cutter? (7)
11 His writing may upset the court he addresses (10)
12 Dry air change making a dicey start (4)
14 Caused annoyance by cutting short? (8)
16 Deliveryman in a hat (6)
17 Note how many react to the Calcutta show? (3)
19 Money earned by opening doors? (6)
21 Flower arrangement might ruin game (8)
24 Spot for some riot assembly (4)
25 Description of a certain sharpness (10)
27 Animal said to be confused with an irregular soldier (7)
28 Cause alarm in stirring fashion (7)
29 Cause of a break when weary of the hard stuff? (5, 7)

DOWN

1 Useful by-product of a cancelled trip? (4-3)
2 Virginia, for instance? (6, 4)
3 Exhausted by the intake? (8)
4 Di puts him on the board (6)
5 One thing you can count on (4)
6 A couple of pence makes a real difference in clothes (7)
7 Settling for what might cause scandal? (12)
10 Offensive reference to one's failing memory? (4, 8)
13 Finding attractions in different directions (10)
15 Not one to eat the same kind (3)
18 The Saint may not be very decisive here (8)
20 Bed on the lake for a certain set (7)
22 Copy it when one friend is around (7)
23 Urge to diminish in favour (6)
26 Guilty or maybe not (4)

1
2
3
4
5
6
7
8
9
10
11
12
13
14
15
16
17
18
19
20
21
22
23
24
25
26
27
28
29

115

ACROSS

6 It provides a certain warmth when one's lying (3, 5, 6)
9 Loved to make a party colourful (6)
10 Falls in with a note on the schedules (8)
11 Honesty hasn't made him what he is (8)
13 Is he dedicated to becoming orange-shaped? (6)
15 It can't be broken if it's undamaged! (6)
17 Go and get a rise (6)
19 There may be one on either side of it (6)
20 A personal interpretation offers no approval (8)
22 Possibly a killer, that heel! (8)
24 Likely to cut up rough? (6)
26 City style presented in good order (7, 7)

DOWN

1 Follow a reverend in opposition? (6, 8)
2 Make a move to cause disturbance (4)
3 Composer of gripping music? (6)
4 Leaves a group with a wayward son (8)
5 He'll be in Aldershot tomorrow (4)
7 Coster around to provide company (6)
8 Not many companions in business? (7, 7)
12 Put down for players? (5)
14 Said to be ahead in urban build-up (5)
16 It's the making of a new fashion (8)
18 Profitable conclusion of a Naval commission (3-3)
21 One tax to cut? (6)
23 Go on to the end (4)
25 Don't put in that Tom and I are involved (4)

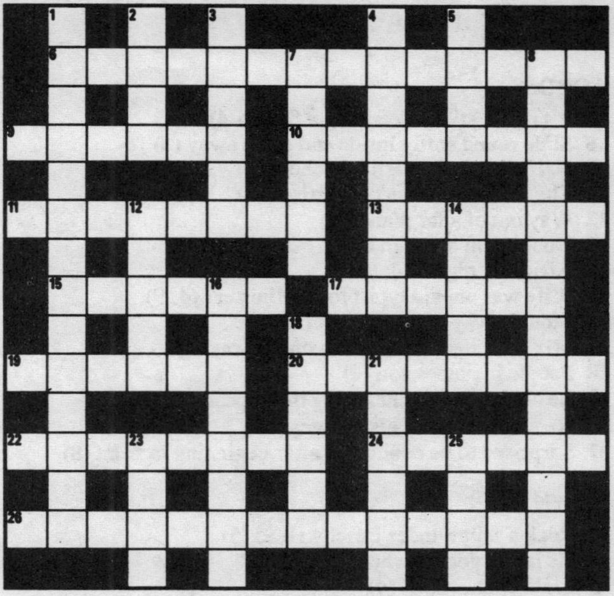
1
2
3
4
5
6
7
8
9
10
11
12
13
14
15
16
17
18
19
20
21
22
23
24
25
26

116

ACROSS

1 It's rather sticky detaining a flier (4-4)
5 Slide round softly inside and drive away (6)
9 Half change the yarn for school (8)
10 The service that isn't advertised (6)
12 Way out of a far planet (4)
13 Nobody invited him to run between (10)
15 Africa by night? (4, 9)
19 Wife was unpaid typist for a Minister? (4, 9)
23 Mouldy way to beat germs (10)
25 Mix with some of the Irish on the way (4)
28 People in possession (6)
29 Be on the way to enhancing the appearance (8)
30 He won't let go of his charges (6)
31 Surprised to be conducted after beginning in front (8)

DOWN

1 Rock a sailor under Beachy Head (6)
2 He hasn't got the whole story (5)
3 Light connection? (4)
4 Stupid error in Room C (7)
6 Descriptive of a show home? (5)
7 Goes in to snoop after a fairy outside and around (9)
8 Able to communicate in letters (8)
11 Edible head (4)
14 Associated with the man in the play (4)
15 Power and income conversion (9)
16 One may put it in to interfere (3)
17 Rebels make a quick start abroad (4)
18 Volume of biography? (8)
20 Lock-up in the battery? (4)
21 Pressing information obtained in the course of getting out (7)
22 Not exactly warm and friendly (6)
24 It just won't go straight (5)
26 It's going to be material (5)
27 Like Clare (4)

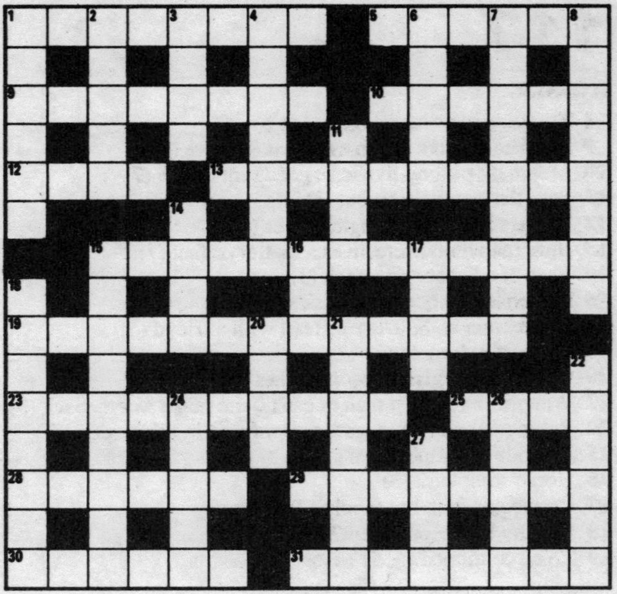

117

ACROSS

1 Stimulating as sentry-go? (11)
9 Weaken resolve to run even around here (7)
10 Merchant putting five in to get a rent return (7)
11 Say, that's quite a horse! (3)
12 Name adapted to a single flower (7)
13 Illuminated real reform as a matter of fact (7)
14 Lout of a lad coming back (3)
15 Understood a pet came back with it (5)
17 Waste time at the Duke's Head with a friend (5)
18 Place of judgment (5)
20 Undertake to give way on clothes (5)
22 Weep when the top man doesn't quite make a comeback (3)
24 Put money on Auntie getting confused in the garden (7)
25 Use rate in simple form (7)
26 Horse complaint (3)
27 Connected with the family (7)
28 Worthy but incompetent? (7)
29 To be continued (6, 5)

DOWN

1 They enlivened the pilgrims' progress (10, 5)
2 One might go up quickly here (7)
3 City subject (5)
4 New writing in a small way? (9)
5 Got fired with a form of dieting (7)
6 Top brass gathered at an international meeting? (7, 8)
7 Sick of being comfortable after a quiet start (6)
8 Get by with a list inside for a rainy day (6)
16 They wouldn't believe her as displaying grit in a car crash (9)
18 They have to be paid by callers (6)
19 No tears for the discomfiture of a statesman (7)
21 Go up, sir, and get a man to show us the dish! (7)
23 Wager about a clergyman getting unpaid rank (6)
25 She's back from her friend's engagement party (5)

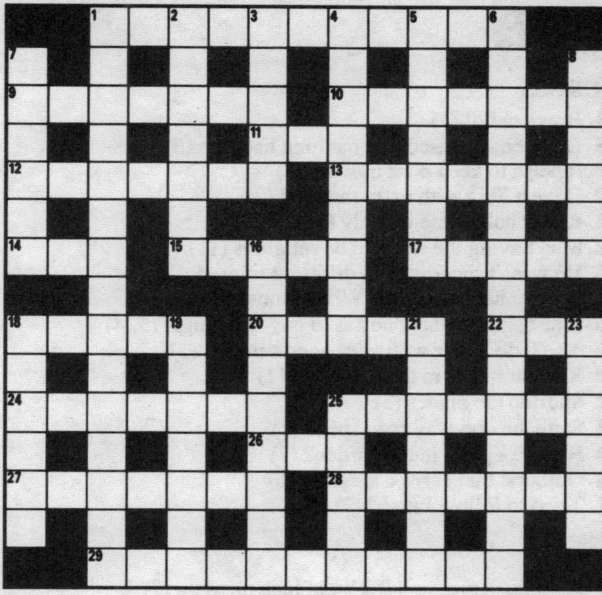
1
2
3
4
5
6
7
8
9
10
11
12
13
14
15
16
17
18
19
20
21
22
23
24
25
26
27
28
29

118

ACROSS

1 Brave child! (7)
5 Don't be surprised if something happens (6)
9 It helps to keep pork moving (7)
10 Have a fling with extra material (7)
11 It may collar one warmly (3)
12 Man having the sense to be religious (11)
13 He wasn't successful in different roles (5)
14 Quiet inhabitant of the White House (9)
16 It just shows what one has to pay for things! (5, 4)
17 You'll do better with very good time off (5)
19 Radiant toil as in the old days (11)
22 Shorten the blades (3)
23 State the one-way road speed (7)
24 Bird-like plant in the garden? (7)
26 Outburst that earns a blessing (6)
27 Tried to follow Lamb? (7)

DOWN

1 Pathetic depression if a bit of luck turns up (7)
2 In a car-port is not change a waste of time? (15)
3 The way to be rather unusual (3)
4 Haunting the Eastern lake (5)
5 Splendidly bright (9)
6 Part of a fork (5)
7 One doesn't feel so guilty after paying it (10, 5)
8 Take a measure in favourite surroundings and have a ball (6)
12 Crowd number (5)
14 It's not granted to everyone (9)
15 Best plan to get capital from Luxembourg (5)
16 Means of sinking one on the green (6)
18 No ground for claiming superiority (7)
20 Foolish gun girl doing the twist (5)
21 Hurry up and find ways to attend (5)
25 Missed opportunity on the road (3)

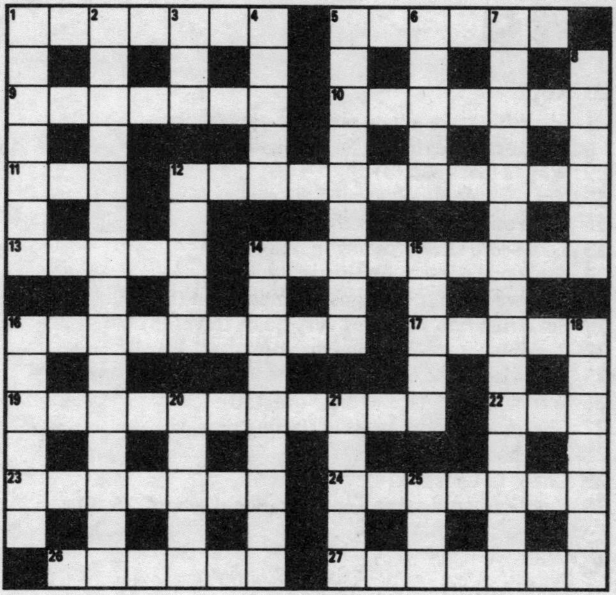

119

ACROSS

1 Something like a light ale? Not very (4, 9)
8 Top person beginning an incantation (4)
9 Way in that's bad (3)
10 Not very alert look around the shelter (6)
11 Chap on the river after dieting? (10)
13 Low score after crossing into Spain (4)
14 Feel compunction for the right bird (6)
16 Throw a chap some signs of amusement (8)
19 Put string into shape for very quick travel (8)
22 Possibly trance-inducing drink (6)
25 Likewise in the news (4)
26 Writer with a place to the North (10)
27 Charm a stubborn beast at starting time (6)
28 For chocolate drinkers? (3)
29 Chaos in Laos too (4)
30 Emotions aroused at a co-educational school? (5, 8)

DOWN

1 God-like hat on the roof ? (7)
2 Go quickly to hell for it? (7)
3 He examines torn epics that could be repaired (9)
4 A place that needs a keeper (3)
5 Nora's turn for wrongdoing (5)
6 Basis for cutting figures (3-4)
7 Write up the music of the planet (7)
12 Revolutionary taken in by a friend providing a knife (7)
15 It might give one a start (3)
17 Sharp, perhaps? It's certainly odd! (9)
18 Bible man starting to be a gay fellow (3)
20 Choose one old lady as the best (7)
21 Not a simple mental stage (7)
23 Some can be sure (7)
24 Works up turbulence in our seas (7)
26 Quoted it among notes (5)
28 Source of the buzz (3)

1 2 3 4 5 6 7
8 9 10
11 12 13
14 15 16 17 18
19 20 21 22 23 24
25 26
27 28 29
30

SOLUTIONS

PUZZLE No. 1

Across: 1, Object lesson. 8, Thermal. 9, Two-step. 11, Co-operator. 12, Solo. 14, Resisted. 16, Contra. 17, Dam. 19, Inkpot. 21, Wistaria. 24, Ibis. 25, Grandstand. 27, Gateway. 28, Gliders. 29, Preparations.
Down: 1, Onerous. 2, Jam session. 3, Collated. 4, Lotion. 5, Slow. 6, Outpost. 7, Stock-raising. 10, Propagandist. 13, Fortissimo. 15, Daw. 18, Midnight. 20, Knitter. 22, Readers. 23, Prayer. 26, Swap.

PUZZLE No. 2

Across: 6, Post-war credits. 9, Closer. 10, Lifelike. 11, Vestment. 13, Upsets. 15, Scrubs. 17, Advice. 19, Liable. 20, Outboard. 22, Incoming. 24, Output. 26, Performing seal.
Down: 1, Applied Science. 2, Isis. 3, Swerve. 4, Profound. 5, Idol. 7, Relate. 8, Take the trouble. 12, Throb. 14, Sligo. 16, Breviary. 18, Mowgli. 21, Trough. 23, Oafs. 25, Then.

PUZZLE No. 3

Across: 1, Contempt. 5, Edicts. 9, Bathroom. 10, Magnet. 12, Lily. 13, Forecaster. 15, Current events. 19, Front entrance. 23, Initiative. 25, Emil. 28, Intone. 29, Moribund. 30, Lyrics. 31, Violence.
Down: 1, Cobalt. 2, Natal. 3, Earl. 4, Promote. 6, Drama. 7, Constance. 8, Satirist. 11, Best. 14, Trot. 15, Chorister. 16, Nut. 17, Vine. 18, Official. 20, Note. 21, Ravioli. 22, Pledge. 24, Ionic. 26, Mourn. 27, Will.

PUZZLE No. 4

Across: 1, Paternalism. 9, Seasons. 10, Treadle. 11, Eli. 12, Inhabit. 13, Peebles. 14, Gas. 15, Ephod. 17, Grain. 18, Panic. 20, Roses. 22, Elm. 24, Incense. 25, Prosper. 26, Wee. 27, Eyewash. 28, Toppers. 29, Manipulated.
Down: 1, Peaches and cream. 2, Trouble. 3, Reset. 4, Antipodes. 5, Iceberg. 6, Middle-age spread. 7, Asking. 8, Person. 16, Horsewhip. 18, Privet. 19, Contain. 21, Shot put. 23, Morose. 25, Petal.

PUZZLE No. 5

Across: 1, Brabant. 5, Accede. 9, Soupcon. 10, Adviser. 11, Ace. 12, Enchantment. 13, Dread. 14, Anchorage. 16, Determine. 17, Fleet. 19, Curtain-call. 22, Lie. 23, Dead-eye. 24, Insight. 26, Decant. 27, Seattle.
Down: 1, Bustard. 2, Amusement arcade. 3, Arc. 4, Tunic. 5, Avalanche. 6, Civet. 7, Desperate plight. 8, Writhe. 12, Elder. 14, Alignment. 15, Offal. 16, Decode. 18, Trestle. 20, Arena. 21, Amiss. 25, Spa.

PUZZLE No. 6

Across: 1, Campaign medal. 8, Enid. 9, Sap. 10, Fruity. 11, Concertina. 13, Maul. 14, Vermin. 16, Cabernet. 19, Crescent. 22, Tights. 25, Anna. 26, Addressees. 27, Gospel. 28, Etc. 29, Able. 30, Football pools.
Down: 1, Console. 2, Modicum. 3,

Assurance. 4, Gap. 5, Mafia. 6, Drummer. 7, Lettuce. 12, Incited. 15, Rue. 17, Buttercup. 18, Noh. 20, Ring off. 21, Shampoo. 23, Gestapo. 24, Trellis. 26, Ad lib. 28, Ell.

PUZZLE No. 7

Across: 1, Disembarking. 8, Overrun. 9, Calling. 11, Ermyntrude. 12, Coma. 14, Undulate. 16, Potent. 17, Sad. 19, Outing. 21, Reproach. 24, Tape. 25, Seminaries. 27, Puccini. 28, Imitate. 29, Olympic Games.
Down: 1, Dreamed. 2, Sprinkling. 3, Minarets. 4, Arcade. 5, Kilt. 6, Noisome. 7, Come out on top. 10, Grantchester. 13, Journalism. 15, Ear. 18, Devising. 20, Topical. 22, Animals. 23, Gemini. 26, Firm.

PUZZLE No. 8

Across: 6, Ungraciousness. 9, Stress. 10, Vanished. 11, Thickset. 13, Accept. 15, Tumble. 17, Wyvern. 19, Willow. 20, Goodness. 22, Abstract. 24, Fallow. 26, Second marriage.
Down: 1, Hunt the thimble. 2, Ogle. 3, Passes. 4, Quandary. 5, Onus. 7, Invite. 8, Stepping-stones. 12, Camel. 14, Clean. 16, Lowlands. 18, Agatha. 21, Offers. 23, Troy. 25, Leap.

PUZZLE No. 9

Across: 1, Hardtack. 5, Pompom. 9, Fearsome. 10, Finnan. 12, Echo. 13, House match. 15, Depressed area. 19, Business hours. 23, Enlistment. 25, Star. 28, Thomas. 29, Literary. 30, Rhymes. 31, Stumbled.
Down: 1, Huffed. 2, Reach. 3, Test. 4, Commode. 6, Opium. 7, Punctures. 8, Minehead. 11, Isis. 14, Span. 15, Desultory. 16, SOS. 17, Dour. 18, Objector. 20, Sump. 21, Hengist. 22, Prayed. 24, Stale. 26, Trail. 27, Term.

PUZZLE No. 10

Across: 1, Straight bat. 9, Upright. 10, Blanket. 11, Egg. 12, Tangier. 13, Oceanic. 14, Ewe. 15, Hotel. 17, Teddy. 18, Sloop. 20, Liner. 22, Cod. 24, Viewing. 25, Appeals. 26, Rap. 27, Niagara. 28, Railing. 29, Elephant gun.
Down: 1, Strange to relate. 2, Roguish. 3, Inter. 4, Hobgoblin. 5, Bravest. 6, Taking dictation. 7, Bustle. 8, Sticky. 16, Telegraph. 18, Saving. 19, Private. 21, Ripping. 23, Design. 25, Apron.

PUZZLE No. 11

Across: 1, Commons. 5, Castle. 9, Extreme. 10, Arrival. 11, Par. 12, Safety-first. 13, Ready. 14, Verminous. 16, Submerged. 17, Giles. 19, Concealment. 22, Two. 23, Refrain. 24, Garment. 26, Statue. 27, Tighten.
Down: 1, Creeper. 2, Material benefit. 3, One. 4, Shelf. 5, Chartered. 6, Serif. 7, Liverpool Street. 8, Plates. 12, Style. 14, Vigilance. 15, Ingot. 16, Secure. 18, Shorten. 20, Exact. 21, Eight. 25, Rig.

PUZZLE No. 12

Across: 1, Scratch player. 8, Gigi. 9, Mat. 10, Toucan. 11, Crosspatch. 13, Gain. 14, Adhere. 16, Beverage. 19, Campbell. 22, Giving. 25, Cage. 26, Foreteller. 27, Repair. 28, Tub. 29, Ally. 30, Rule of the road.
Down: 1, Stirred. 2, Reissue. 3, Timepiece. 4, Hit. 5, Latch. 6, Younger. 7, Reading. 12, Tubular. 15, Hum. 17, Vegetable. 18, Ali. 20, Amateur. 21, Prevail. 23, Volcano. 24, Needled. 26, Forgo. 28, Tot.

PUZZLE No. 13

Across: 1, Turn of phrase. 8, Nanette. 9, Parsnip. 11, Prevailing. 12, Stop. 14, Constant. 16, Bearer. 17, Dab. 19, Option. 21, Panorama. 24, Amen. 25, Displacing. 27, Embrace. 28, Tuition. 29, Veiled threat.
Down: 1, Tintern. 2, Retraction. 3, Overland. 4, Piping. 5, Rare. 6, Senator. 7, Inspectorate. 10, Paper-hanging. 13, Decorative. 15, Tap. 18, Bad patch. 20, Tremble. 22, Animist. 23, Gilead. 26, Wall.

PUZZLE No. 14

Across: 6, Changing places. 9, Joshua. 10, Platonic. 11, Sprinter. 13, Entity. 15, In fact. 17, Strain. 19, Shorts. 20, Artistic. 22, Dead-head. 24, Wangle. 26, Standing orders.

Down: 1, Accomplishment. 2, Wash. 3, Aghast. 4, Apparent. 5, Mayo. 7, Napery. 8, Existentialist. 12, Infer. 14, Traps. 16, Cosmetic. 18, Lapdog. 21, Toward. 23, Done. 25, Need.

PUZZLE No. 15

Across: 1, Bird-cage. 5, Corset. 9, Carnival. 10, Stroll. 12, Loll. 13, Four-poster. 15, Contradiction. 19, One-day cricket. 23, Impoverish. 25, Stir. 28, Idiocy. 29, Armagnac. 30, Spells. 31, Advanced.

Down: 1, Buckle. 2, Rural. 3, Clip. 4, Glamour. 6, Outdo. 7, Short list. 8, Tolerant. 11, Grid. 14, Anna. 15, Cheapside. 16, Air. 17, Cake. 18, Politics. 20, Cart. 21, Insured. 22, Graced. 24, Vocal. 26, Tonic. 27, Cana.

PUZZLE No. 16

Across: 1, Sailor's knot. 9, Express. 10, Uttered. 11, Tip. 12, Surpass. 13, Parquet. 14, Moo. 15, Defer. 17, Lehar. 18, Snoop. 20, Rider. 22, Arm. 24, Inferno. 25, Cabaret. 26, Two. 27, Lockout. 28, Plumage. 29, Roman candle.

Down: 1, Superior officer. 2, Iceland. 3, Ousts. 4, Scuppered. 5, Natural. 6, Through carriage. 7, Jetsam. 8, Editor. 16, Forgotten. 18, Spills. 19, Perform. 21, Rebound. 23, Mutter. 25, Copra.

PUZZLE No. 17

Across: 1, Refuses. 5, Wrench. 9, Shopper. 10, Triplet. 11, RAF. 12, Low pressure. 13, Moron. 14, Anarchism. 16, Potential. 17, Regal. 19, Emotionally. 22, Art. 23, Transit. 24, Lighter. 26, Attend. 27, Central.

Down: 1, Rostrum. 2, From first to last. 3, Sup. 4, Straw. 5, Waterfall. 6, Emits. 7, Colouring matter. 8, Stream. 12, Linen. 14, Alienated. 15, Carry. 16, Pretty. 18, Literal. 20, Issue. 21, Lilac. 25, Gun.

PUZZLE No. 18

Across: 1, Treat like dirt. 8, Rice. 9, Ilk. 10, Locker. 11, Soft-spoken. 13, Each. 14, Middle. 16, Thickset. 19, Japanese. 22, Superb. 25, Odds. 26, Restricted. 27, Stoned. 28, Pub. 29, Area. 30, Ruling passion.

Down: 1, Tripoli. 2, Elected. 3, Tailpiece. 4, Irk. 5, Ellen. 6, In check. 7, Treacle. 12, Kittens. 15, Dip. 17, Inscribes. 18, See. 20, Auditor. 21, Arsenal. 23, Peccavi. 24, Roedean. 26, Rodin. 28, Pip.

PUZZLE No. 19

Across: 1, Reform school. 8, Maigret. 9, Piastre. 11, Extortions. 12, Moor. 14, Stranger. 16, Livery. 17, Rap. 19, Rudder. 21, Fantasia. 24, Back. 25, Toleration. 27, Evasive. 28, Anglian. 29, Amphitheatre.

Down: 1, Roister. 2, Forerunner. 3, Retailer. 4, Supine. 5, Hear. 6, Outcome. 7, Immeasurable. 10, Early warning. 13, Distraught. 15, RAF. 18, Pale-face. 20, Declaim. 22, Suicide. 23, Molest. 26, Wish.

PUZZLE No. 20

Across: 6, On with the dance. 9, Amanda. 10, Bachelor. 11, Intruder. 13, Excise. 15, Rag-man. 17, Stowed. 19, Gazebo. 20, Taffrail. 22, Idolater. 24, Resign. 26, Under the hammer.

Down: 1, Common or garden. 2, Swan. 3, Strand. 4, Sea-chest. 5, Fare. 7, Tabard. 8, Crossed fingers. 12, Rogue 14, Cower. 16, Apostate. 18, Starve. 21, Formal. 23, Lien. 25, Some.

PUZZLE No. 21

Across: 1, Knapsack. 5, Catnip. 9, Detailed. 10, Buffer. 12, Aura. 13, Indentured. 15, Strip cartoons. 19, Touch one's toes. 23, Exhaustive. 25, Slip. 28, Myopic. 29, Inclined. 30, Retina. 31, Hypnosis.

Down: 1, Kidnap. 2, Alter. 3, Snip.

4, Clean up. 6, Adult. 7, Nefarious. 8, Parodist. 11, Beta. 14, Arch. 15, Southport. 16, Cue. 17, Took. 18, Streamer. 20, Note. 21, Seventy. 22, Spades. 24, Union. 26, Lines. 27, Plan.

PUZZLE No. 22

Across: 1, Bear witness. 9, Assigns. 10, Magneto. 11, Tab. 12, Confine. 13, Stipend. 14, SOS. 15, Hippo. 17, Hefty. 18, Remit. 20, Press. 22, Hop. 24, Pit-head. 25, Polecat. 26, Rue. 27, Twosome. 28, America. 29, Storm-centre.
Down: 1, Business methods. 2, Anguish. 3, Waste. 4, Tombstone. 5, English. 6, Scene of the crime. 7, Dances. 8, Lordly. 16, Pipe-dream. 18, Repute. 19, Tremolo. 21, Solvent. 23, Potman. 25, Peace.

PUZZLE No. 23

Across: 1, Endowed. 5, Wigwam. 9, Equable. 10, Trapper. 11, All. 12, Compressing. 13, Toque. 14, Crankcase. 16, Whitebait. 17, Amiss. 19, Acknowledge. 22, Nun. 23, Trident. 24, Explode. 26, Beaten. 27, Shrimps.
Down: 1, Elegant. 2, Double-quick time. 3, Web. 4, Dream. 5, Water-cart. 6, Grass. 7, Application form. 8, Brogue. 12, Crewe. 14, Charlatan. 15, Knave. 16, Wealth. 18, Singers. 20, Overt. 21, Dress. 25, Par.

PUZZLE No. 24

Across: 1, Knock for knock. 8, Wend. 9, Tub. 10, Ebbing. 11, Near-misses. 13, Tome. 14, Stadia. 16, Nestling. 19, Stampede. 22, Access. 25, Lift. 26, Armigerous. 27, Combat. 28, Pet. 29, Brag. 30, French perfume.
Down: 1, Keenest. 2, Ordered. 3, Kittiwake. 4, Orb. 5, Knees. 6, Orbital. 7, Kinsman. 12, Sunbeam. 15, Ada. 17, Slaughter. 18, Ice. 20, Tail off. 21, Mutable. 23, Caribou. 24, Sausage. 26, Attic. 28, Pop.

PUZZLE No. 25

Across: 1, Expectations. 8, Initial. 9, Chirrup. 11, Foretastes. 12, Home. 14, Remedial. 16, Lassie. 17, Law. 19, Nimbus. 21, Carapace. 24, Iona. 25, Quantities. 27, Lurched. 28, Chester. 29, Manufacturer.
Down: 1, Epigram. 2, Pointed out. 3, Colossal. 4, Archer. 5, Iris. 6, Nervous. 7, Differential. 10, Predecessors. 13, Carabineer. 15, Lac. 18, Wainscot. 20, Minerva. 22, Aviator. 23, Tundra. 26, Thou.

PUZZLE No. 26

Across: 6, Pull the strings. 9, Dragon. 10, Aversion. 11, Steamers. 13, Ground. 15, Fiends. 17, Chilli. 19, Shades. 20, Scratchy. 22, Calabria. 24, Barrow. 26, Hell-fire Corner.
Down: 1, Spirit of the age. 2, flag. 3, Stance. 4, Strength. 5, Bias. 7, Elapse. 8, Good neighbours. 12, Amend. 14, Owlet. 16, Distrait. 18, Escape. 21, Ribbon. 23, Ally. 25, Rung.

PUZZLE No. 27

Across: 1, Clansman. 5, Dotard. 9, Resolute. 10, Mirage. 12, Free. 13, Firebricks. 15, Family feeling. 19, Superabundant. 23, Iridescent. 25, Safe. 28, Aghast. 29, Stiletto. 30, Trying. 31, Upper cut.
Down: 1, Carafe. 2, Aisle. 3, Salt. 4, Ant-hill. 6, Osier. 7, Anarchist. 8, Dressage. 11, Beef. 14, Omar. 15, Foppishly. 16, You. 17, Exam. 18, Aspirant. 20, Back. 21, Non-stop. 22, Report. 24, Essen. 26, Attic. 27, Blue.

PUZZLE No. 28

Across: 1, Story-teller. 9, Erratic. 10, Cleaver. 11, Hoe. 12, Consort. 13, Lobelia. 14, Ems. 15, Title. 17, Dotty. 18, Delve. 20, Satyr. 22, Ova. 24, Pandora. 25, Actuate. 26, Man. 27, Combine. 28, Gunning. 29, None the less.
Down: 1, Strong silent man. 2, Outpost. 3, Yacht. 4, Excellent. 5, Lie-abed. 6, Revolutionaries. 7, Rescue. 8, Greasy. 16, Testament. 18, Depict. 19, Emotion. 21, Retinue. 23, Avenge. 25, Angle.

PUZZLE No. 29

Across: 1, Bath-tub. 5, Recall. 9, Unknown. 10, Scatter. 11, Ski. 12, Thunderclap. 13, Drown. 14, Innocuous. 16, Interlude. 17, Inner. 19, Overbidding. 22, Tom. 23, Athwart. 24, Arabian. 26, Intend. 27, Eclogue.
Down: 1, Bruised. 2, Take it on the chin. 3, Two. 4, Bantu. 5, Residence. 6, Chair. 7, Little or nothing. 8, Gropes. 12, Tenor. 14, Inundated. 15, Cling. 16, Isobar. 18, Romance. 20, Brave. 21, Image. 25, Awl.

PUZZLE No. 30

Across: 1, Precious metal. 8, Oral. 9, Sun. 10, Goings. 11, Conversant. 13, Tray. 14, Seance. 16, Gathered. 19, Omelette. 22, Offers. 25, Adam. 26, Resistance. 27, Screen. 28, Tie. 29, Goon. 3O, Mother country.
Down: 1, Purpose. 2, Enliven. 3, Insurgent. 4, Urn. 5, Might. 6, Thistle. 7, Luggage. 12, Algiers. 15, Abe. 17, Trousseau. 18, Rye. 20, Modicum. 21, Lambent. 23, Fraught. 24, Rectory. 26, Range. 28, Tic.

PUZZLE No. 31

Across: 1, Implications. 8, Entreat. 9, Soprano. 11, Lineaments. 12, Leaf. 14, Abdullah. 16, Hectic. 17, Gas. 19, Extent. 21, Sprinter. 24, Idea. 25, Meerschaum. 27, Noodles. 28, Raiders. 29, Colonel Bogey.
Down: 1, Intoned. 2, Prevailing. 3, In the bag. 4, Assets. 5, Impi. 6, Nearest. 7, Tell-tale sign. 10, Officers' mess. 13, Bewitching. 15, Has. 18, Spare-rib. 20, Tremolo. 22, Tracery. 23, Tessie. 26, Alto.

PUZZLE No. 32

Across: 6, Unique occasion. 9, Closet. 10,Nauseate. 11, Indolent. 13, Litter. 15, Trauma. 17, Estate. 19, Ordeal. 20, Engender. 22, Customer. 24, Apache. 26, Shooting season.
Down: 1, Pulling through. 2, Miss. 3, Bustle. 4, Scruples. 5, Isle. 7, Ornate. 8, On the telephone. 12, Orate. 14, Train. 16, Milkmaid. 18, Red rag. 21, Gravel. 23, Tool. 25, Apse.

PUZZLE No. 33

Across: 1, Foreword. 5, Combat. 9, Bedstead. 10, Stroke. 12, Item. 13, Sideboards. 15, Paint stripper. 19, Revolutionary. 23, Admittance. 25, Asia. 28, Genial. 29, Manifold. 30, Duster. 3l, Addendum.
Down: 1, Fabric. 2, Ridge. 3, Wits. 4, Realist. 6, Outdo. 7, Biography. 8, Treasury. 11, Kent. 14, Bill. 15, Pavements. 16, Ski. 17, Ivan. 18, Arranged. 20, Teak. 21, Orchard. 22, Random. 24, Trade. 26, Sword. 27, Rife.

PUZZLE No. 34

Across: 1, Waiting list. 9, Trivial. 10, Neatest. 11, Eft. 12, Collier. 13, Let down. 14, Sun. 15, Locum. 17, Yokes. 18, Medoc. 20, Ernie. 22, Owl. 24, Parsnip. 25, Broiler. 26, Ado. 27, Raiment. 28, Twiddle. 29, Half a chance.
Down: 1, Whirling Dervish. 2, Initial. 3, Idler. 4, Gentlemen. 5, Inaptly. 6, Tree of knowledge. 7, Stocks. 8, Stones. 16, Cleopatra. 18, Mopers. 19, Conceal. 21, Emotion. 23, Larder. 25, Botch.

PUZZLE No. 35

Across: 1, Diverts. 5, Brutes. 9, Balance. 10, Topical. 11, Tea. 12, Infantryman. 13, Rufus. 14, Institute. 16, Graceless. 17, Idiom. 19, Outbuilding. 22, All. 23, Profits. 24, Fission. 26, Ascend. 27, Romance.
Down: 1, Debater. 2, Vulgar fractions. 3, Run. 4, Shelf. 5, Botanists. 6, Upper. 7, Excommunication. 8, Glance. 12, Issue. 14, Idealised. 15, Icing. 16, Groups. 18, Melanie. 20, Unite. 21, Infer. 25, Sum.

PUZZLE No. 36

Across: 1, Unforeseeable. 8, Diva. 9, Hop. 10, Height. 11, Postmaster. 13, Arcs. 14, Smarts. 16, Recently. 19, Dislodge. 22, Latest. 25, Stir. 26, Proverbial. 27, Archer. 28, Bad. 29, Exit. 30, Middlesbrough.
Down: 1, Uniform. 2, flatter. 3,

Rehearsed. 4, Sip. 5, Ether. 6, Britain. 7, Ethical. 12, Torpedo. 15, Ass. 17, Callender. 18, Tie. 20, Interim. 21, Lurched. 23, Tableau. 24, Slavish. 26, Peril. 28, Bus.

PUZZLE No. 37

Across: 1, Prescription. 8, Overall. 9, Swallow. 11, Traditions. 12, Lava. 14, Overturn. 16, Severe. 17, Sip. 19, Editor. 21, Left half. 24, Exam. 25, Fraudulent. 27, Thicket. 28, Amalgam. 29, United States.
Down: 1, Preface. 2, Emaciation. 3, Colliers. 4, Insane. 5, Team. 6, Oil-cake. 7, Postponement. 10, Whale of a time. 13, Restaurant. 15, Nil. 18, Petulant. 20, Italian. 22, Avenges. 23, Grated. 26, Skit.

PUZZLE No. 38

Across: 6, Cambridgeshire. 9, Quetta. 10, Positive. 11, Eyeglass. 13, Notary. 15, Norman. 17, Plunge. 19, Effect. 20, Mistrial. 22, Proposal. 24, Bandit. 26, Deregistration.
Down: 1, Occupying force. 2, Smut. 3, Armada. 4, Personal. 5, Shot. 7, Depose. 8, Reverberations. 12, Gorge. 14, Tenor. 16, Artistic. 18, Amulet. 21, Subway. 23, Pier. 25, Nail. .

PUZZLE No. 39

Across: 1, Hard luck. 5, Cactus. 9, Solitary. 10, Chaste. 12, Lack. 13, Contingent. 15, Pressure gauge. 19, Infringements. 23, Brandishes. 25, Anna. 28, Radial. 29, Dividend. 30, Dorcas. 31, Egg-shell.
Down: 1, Hustle. 2, Relic. 3, Late. 4, Curious. 6, Ashen. 7, Taste-buds. 8, Sheathed. 11, Star. 14, Semi. 15, Puff-adder. 16, Use. 17, Gang. 18, Timbered. 20, Gust. 21, Meeting. 22, Sandal. 24, Diana. 26, Niece. 27, Kiss.

PUZZLE No. 40

Across: 1, The whole hog. 9, Anoraks. 10, Nominal. 11, End. 12, Dilated. 13, Strolls. 14, Rev. 15, Casca. 17, Camps. 18, Darts. 20, Anent. 22, Nut. 24, Maypole. 25, Mermaid. 26, Cue. 27, Traitor. 28, Drummer. 29, Fine weather.
Down: 1, Too clever by half. 2, Elastic. 3, Hosed. 4, Landscape. 5, Homeric. 6, Gentleman farmer. 7, Gander. 8, Flasks. 16, Scarecrow. 18, Dimity. 19, Shorten. 21, Through. 23, Tudors. 25, Media.

PUZZLE No.41

Across: 1, Violent. 5, Orchid. 9, Let down. 10, Snifter. 11, Alf. 12, Vicar of Bray. 13, Other. 14, Freemason. 16, Newcomers. 17, Guess. 19, Paying guest. 22, Pro. 23, Exploit. 24, Gagarin. 26, Attend. 27, Essayed.
Down: 1, Volcano. 2, Out-of-the way spot. 3, Ego. 4, Tonic. 5, Observers. 6, Cliff. 7, Interested party. 8, Crayon. 12, Virgo. 14, Freighted. 15, Might. 16, Napper. 18, Scorned. 20, Noose. 21, Eagle. 25, Gas.

PUZZLE No. 42.

Across: 1, Cock of the walk. 8, Inca. 9, Cap. 10, Granta. 11, Counteract. 13, Echo. 14, Amulet. 16, Tolerant. 19, Italians. 22, Matter. 25, Stab. 26, Songstress. 27, Angler. 28, Bug. 29, Acre. 30, Changing rooms.
Down: 1, Conform. 2, Channel. 3, Orchestra. 4, Tip. 5, Eight. 6, Amateur. 7, Kitchen. 12, Artisan. 15, USA. 17, Lump-sugar. 18, Apt. 20, Titanic. 21, Lobelia. 23, Tornado. 24, Ensures. 26, Shrug. 28, Ben.

PUZZLE No. 43.

Across: 1, Amazing Grace. 8, Roasted. 9, Purview. 11, Meticulous. 12, Cape. 14, Sidelong. 16, Ordeal. 17, Tap. 19, Digits. 21, Brewster. 24, Away. 25, Confessing. 27, Dialect. 28, Egotist. 29, Man of Mystery.
Down: 1, Adapted. 2, Articulate. 3, Indolent. 4, Gypsum. 5, Rare. 6, Climate. 7, Promised Land. 10, Wheelwrights. 13, Brown stone. 15, Gab. 18, Proffers. 20, Granada. 22, Trinity. 23, Bottom. 26, Veto.

PUZZLE No. 44

Across: 6, Hold your horses. 9,

Rowena. 10, Envelope. 11, Stations. 13, Nature. 15, Eating. 17, Esteem. 19, Wallop. 20, Argument. 22, Emphatic. 24, Outlay. 26, Orchestra stall.
Down: 1, Throw the hammer. 2, Blue. 3, Dynamo. 4, Shavings. 5, Oral. 7, Uneasy. 8, Experimentally. 12, Total. 14, Therm. 16, Nepotism. 18, Dancer. 2l, Grouse. 23, Ha-ha. 25, Tram.

PUZZLE No. 45

Across: 1, Accolade. 5 Stupor. 9, Forecast. 10, Sarong. 12, Rule. 13, Carnations. 15, Mountain range. 19, Circumference. 23, Associated. 25, Opal. 28, Boiler. 29, Quantity. 30, Exempt. 31, Skin deep.
Down: 1, Afford. 2, Carol. 3, Lick. 4, Descant. 6, Trait. 7, Pronounce. 8, Register. 11, Anti. 14, Lulu. 15, Marks time. 16, Ace. 17, Rank. 18, Scramble. 20, Flaw. 21, Roebuck. 22, Play up. 24, Creep. 26, Poise. 27, Anon.

PUZZLE No. 46

Across: 1, Modern dress. 9, Ongoing. 10, Flapper. 11, Use. 12, Gazette. 13, Retired. 14, Tan. 15, Rosie. 17, Drone. 18, Music. 20, Outer. 22, Ice. 24, Declaim. 25, Assists. 26, Asp. 27, Evident. 28, Pottery. 29, Naughty Word.
Down: 1, Magazine section. 2, Drifter. 3, Rogue. 4, Deferment. 5, Exacted. 6, Supersonic speed. 7, Bought. 8, Bridge. 16, Slow-match. 18, Madder. 19, Chateau. 21, Risotto. 23, Essays. 25, Apply.

PUZZLE No. 47

Across: 1, Nippers. 5, Scouse. 9, Nicosia. 10, Theorem. 11, Tea. 12, Inheritance. 13, Piece. 14, Technique. 16, Shortfall. 17, Least. 19, Elizabethan. 22, Tub. 23, Cranium. 24, Visitor. 26, Astern. 27, Regress.
Down: 1, Non-stop. 2, Package holidays. 3, Ems. 4, Smash. 5, Satirical. 6, Overt. 7, String quartette. 8, Impede. 12, Inept. 14, Tradesman. 15, Nylon. 16, Speech. 18, Tabards. 20, Alice. 21, Hover. 25, Sag.

PUZZLE No. 48

Across: 1, Luminous paint. 8, Aver. 9, Ink. 10, Resent. 11, Breathless. 13, Earl. 14, Studio. 16, Prettily. 19, Converse. 22, Prints. 25, Star. 26, Assurances. 27, Amount. 28, Pen. 29, Back. 30, Musical comedy.
Down: 1, Leveret. 2, Mermaid. 3, Neighbour. 4, Usk. 5, Paris. 6, Inspect. 7, Tendril. 12, Express. 15, Urn. 17, Esperanto. 18, Ian. 20, Optimum. 21, Virtues. 23, Ignoble. 24, Treacly. 26, Attic. 28, Pal.

PUZZLE No. 49

Across: 1, Pitch and toss. 8, Auction. 9, Mantrap. 11, Epitomised. 12, Lima. 14, Bohemian. 16, Urgent. 17, Pal. 19, Armada. 21, Baccarat. 24, Iron. 25, Didgeridoo. 27, Gallant. 28, Article. 29, Stormy petrel.
Down: 1, Puckish. 2, Tailor-made. 3, Handicap. 4, Number. 5, Tent. 6, Service. 7, Take a beating. 10, Practitioner. 13, Procurator. 15, Nab. 18, Language. 20, Moonlit. 22, Radical. 23, Wintry. 26, Hair.

PUZZLE No. 50

Across: 6, Misappropriate. 9, Domain. 10, Carnival. 11, Stampede. 13, Thrush. 15, Notion. 17, Cresta. 19, Defect. 20, Register. 22, Verbiage. 24, Attack. 26, Straight as a die.
Down: 1, Important event. 2, Asia. 3, Sponge. 4, Operator. 5, Gigi. 7, Rocket. 8, Transparencies. 12, Mitre. 14, Roses. 16, Outrange. 18, Arrest. 21, Glassy. 23, Beat. 25, Tidy.

PUZZLE No. 51

Across: 1, Highball. 5, Swipes. 9, Trickery. 10, Stolen. 12; Even. 13, Slaughters. 15, Booking-office. 19, Discount store. 23, Roof-garden. 25, Will. 28, Barrow. 29, Minority. 30, Excess. 31, Old-timer.
Down: 1, Hither. 2, Guise. 3, Bake 4, Lorelei. 6, Witch. 7, Pulverise. 8, Sinister. 11, Rung. 14, Solo. 15, Bishopric. 16, Nut. 17, Flow. 18, Adorable. 20, Nark. 21, Special. 22, Player. 24, Gross. 26, Idiom. 27, Bolt.

PUZZLE No. 52

Across: 1, Pomegranate. 9, Balance. 10, Classic. 11, Exe. 12, Scoured. 13, Reaumur. 14, Due. 15, Hosea. 17, Traps. 18, Disco. 20, Venus. 22, Era. 24, Lectern. 25, Sell-out. 26, Tot. 27, Absolve. 28, Anagram. 29, Pay increase.
Down: 1, Pull one's socks up. 2, Monarch. 3, Greed. 4, Ascertain. 5, Adamant. 6, Epsom racecourse. 7, Abused. 8, Scores. 16, Seventeen. 18, Dollar. 19, Overlay. 21, Sultana. 23, Asthma. 25, Stair.

PUZZLE No. 53

Across: 1, Newgate. 5, Prague. 9, Titania. 10, Emended. 11, Ash. 12, Close secret. 13, Liner. 14, Furnished. 16, Exhausted. 17, Arson. 19, Permanently. 22, Rag. 23, Reigned. 24, Compact. 26, Peeled. 27, Tannery.
Down: 1, Netball. 2, Watch on the Rhine. 3, Ann. 4, Erato. 5, Preferred. 6, Adele. 7, Under the surface. 8, Edited. 12, Corfu. 14, Fat-headed. 15, Italy. 16, Export. 18, Nightly. 20, Annul. 21, Tacit. 25, Man.

PUZZLE No. 54

Across: 1, Weight-lifting. 8, Boss. 9, Use. 10, Client. 11, Deliveries. 13, Iris. 14, Gazebo. 16, Ash-plant. 19, Deportee. 22, Deodar. 25, Beta. 26, Drysaltery. 27, Lariat. 28, Bag. 29, Oboe. 30, Leather-jacket.
Down: 1, Woomera. 2, Inspire. 3, House-boat. 4, Lie. 5, Facts. 6, Initial. 7, Gentian. 12, Imagery. 15, Zip. 17, Hydrangea. 18, Aid. 20, Eyeball. 21, Ocarina. 23, Outlook. 24, Airport. 26, Dutch. 28, Bar.

PUZZLE No. 55

Across: 1, Prescription. 8, Accepts. 9, Conceal. 11, Co-ordinate. 12, Limb. 14, Adoptive. 16, Smoker. 17, Alb. 19, Doctor. 21, Funereal. 24, Alan. 25, Sailmakers. 27, Dearest. 28, Tuition. 29, Belly-dancers.
Down: 1, Piccolo. 2, Expedition. 3, Casanova. 4, Incite. 5, Tank. 6, Obelisk. 7, Watch and ward. 10, Liberalising. 13, Imperative. 15, Elf. 18, Bulletin. 20, Charade. 22, Enemies. 23, Parted. 26, Well.

PUZZLE No. 56

Across: 1, Turkish delight. 9, Tivoli. 10, Failings. 11, Strangle. 13, Occult. 15, Alight. 17, Decamp. 19, Recess. 20, Imperils. 22, Wheatear. 24, Clause. 26, Sweeping glance.
Down: 1, Strip-tease show. 2, Brio. 3, Living. 4, Seminole. 5, Mimi. 7, Huffed. 8, Highly polished. 12, Alive. 14, Chair. 16, Hysteria. 18, Oil-rig. 21, Pickle. 23, Apex. 25, Aunt.

PUZZLE No. 57

Across: 1, Foremost. 5, Gallop. 9, Contempt. 10, Colour. 12, Open. 13, Reassessed. 15, Professionals. 19, Turn off the tap. 23, Iron-master. 25, Scab. 28, Pompom. 29, Mitigate. 30, Darken. 31, Ignorant.
Down: 1, Factor. 2, Range. 3, Mien. 4, Supreme. 6, Alone. 7, Look sharp. 8, Parodist. 11, Asks. 14, Solo. 15, Performer. 16, Set. 17, Oath. 18, Stripped. 20, Fist. 21, Heeling. 22, Object. 24, Moose. 26, Clara. 27, Silo.

PUZZLE No. 58

Across: 1, Extradition. 9, Burgess. 10, Elector. 11, Awl. 12, Anybody. 13, Actions. 14 Nun. 15, Lucid. 17, Araby. 18, Gamma. 20, Arras. 22, Ham. 24, Air-base. 25, Leaflet. 26, Lea. 27, Climate. 28, Paladin. 29, Get under way.
Down: 1, Early one morning. 2, Trefoil. 3, Assay. 4, Icelander. 5, Inertia. 6, National holiday. 7, Obtain. 8, Crusty. 16, Chameleon. 18, Glance. 19, Adamant. 21, Shallow. 23, Mating. 25, Lapse.

PUZZLE No. 59

Across: 1, Durable. 5, Potash. 9, Suspect. 10, Elevate. 11, Air. 12, Convertible. 13, Fleet. 14, Fortnight. 16, Watchword. 17, Tango. 19,

Projections. 22, Ice. 23, Timpani. 24, Rebuild. 26, Sneeze. 27, Strayed.
Down: 1, Distaff. 2, Resurrection-man. 3, Bee. 4, Eaten. 5, Preferred. 6, Trent. 7, Shabby gentility. 8, Cement. 12, Catch. 14, Frost-bite. 15, Notes. 16, Wapiti. 18, Overdid. 20, Evade. 21, Ogres. 25, Bar.

PUZZLE No. 60

Across: 1, Jekyll and Hyde. 8, Asia. 9, Ram. 10, Stupid. 11, Dispensary. 13, Glow. 14, Secret. 16, Discreet. 19, Unscrews. 22, Bundle. 25, Burn. 26, Confidence. 27, Cinema. 28, Dai. 29, Lien. 30, Hunting season.
Down: 1, Justice. 2, Knapper. 3, Lorgnette. 4, Arm. 5, Dusty. 6, Younger. 7, Episode. 12, Addison. 15, Cos. 17, Subsidise. 18, End. 20, Nourish. 21, Concern. 23, Needles. 24, Lectern. 26, Coati. 28, Dig.

PUZZLE No. 61

Across: 1, Appertaining. 8, Moaners. 9, Develop. 11, Ridiculous. 12, View. 14, Vendetta. 16, Sawyer. 17, Err. 19, Detect. 21, Mistreat. 24, Nine. 25, Preferment. 27, Element. 28, Avocado. 29, Running fight.
Down: 1, Abandon. 2, Prescience. 3, Resolute. 4, Ardour. 5, Navy. 6, Nullity. 7, Improvidence. 10, Power station. 13, Patter-song. 15, Arm. 18, Riff-raff. 20, Tonneau. 22, Elegant. 23, Proton. 26, Bean.

PUZZLE No. 62

Across: 6, Prince Charming. 9, Gamble. 10, Meantime. 11, Begrudge. 13, Absent. 15, Sparse. 17, Thrill. 19, Cotton. 20, Overhead. 22, Incident. 24, Cabman. 26, Triple alliance.
Down: 1, Speakers' Corner. 2, Limb. 3, Screed. 4, Calabash. 5, Smut. 7, Comber. 8, Nominal damages. 12, React. 14, Smith. 16, Sundered. 18, Mortal. 21, Euclid. 23, Impi. 25, Bank.

PUZZLE No. 63

Across: 1, Lame duck. 5, Baltic. 9, Salutary. 10, Stamen. 12, Nine. 13, Wage freeze. 15, Balance in hand. 19, Comprehensive. 23, Adam's apple. 25, True. 28, Button. 29, Disaster. 30, Escort. 31, Sycamore.
Down: 1, Losing. 2, Melon. 3, Duty. 4, Curtain. 6, Attar. 7, Temperate. 8, Contends. 11, Here. 14, Slur. 15, Bombastic. 16, Cue. 17, Nail. 18, Scramble. 20, Hope. 21, Nullity. 22, Degree. 24, Spoor. 26, Ratio. 27, Data.

PUZZLE No. 64

Across: 1, Wrong number. 9, Adaptor. 10, Detects. 11, Bee. 12, Schools. 13, Remorse. 14, Tor. 15, Torso. 17, Niece. 18, Ashes. 20, Chess. 22, Mud. 24, Beseech. 25, Classic. 26, Oil. 27, Stopper. 28, Animate. 29, Market-place.
Down: 1, Weather the storm. 2, Outpost. 3, Garbs. 4, Underdone. 5, Batsman. 6, Recorded message. 7, Basset. 8, Essene. 16, Racehorse. 18, Ambush. 19, Sleeper. 21, Stamina. 23, Docker. 25, Clasp.

PUZZLE No. 65

Across: 1, Perfect. 5, Policy. 9, Arcadia. 10, Abdomen. 11, Tip. 12, Brainwashed. 13, Child. 14, Programme. 16, Cantering. 17, Votes. 19, Spectacular. 22, Run. 23, Outcrop. 24, Gamboge. 26, Gerbil. 27, Thistle.
Down: 1, Plastic. 2, Reception centre. 3, End. 4, Tiara. 5, Plainsong. 6, Lydia. 7, Come home to roost. 8, On edge. 12, Badge. 14, Principal. 15, Rover. 16, Castor. 18, Sincere. 20, Throb. 21, Light. 25, Mai.

PUZZLE No. 66

Across: 1, With both hands. 8, Anna. 9, Urn. 10, Saturn. 11, Confidence. 13, Riot. 14, Rescue. 16, Modelled. 19, Stressed. 22, Subway. 25, Snug. 26, Secretaire. 27, Debate. 28, Ova. 29, Trip. 30, Unenforceable.
Down: 1, Winsome. 2, Traffic. 3, Boundless. 4, Tin. 5, Haste. 6, Natural. 7, Scrooge. 12, Nomadic. 15, Sir. 17, Desperate. 18, Low. 20, Tonneau. 21, Engrave. 23, Bran-tub. 24, Air-line. 26, Shelf. 28, Oar.

PUZZLE No. 67

Across: 1, Faith-healers. 8, Adapted 9, Twin-set. 11, Experience. 12, Step. 14, Furbelow. 16, Got off. 17, Was. 19, Coffer. 21, Dispatch. 24, Tank. 25, Aide-de-camp. 27, Hundred. 28, Initial. 29, Remote chance.

Down: 1, Flapper. 2, Intervened. 3, Hedgerow. 4, Entice. 5, Lair. 6, Risotto. 7, Case of Scotch. 10, Top of the poll. 13, Completion. 15, Wad. 18, Side-dish. 20, Finance. 22, Tea-time. 23, Middle. 26, Ergo.

PUZZLE No. 68

Across: 6, Character study. 9, Unreal. 10, Imperial. 11, Dramatic. 13, Sprays. 15, Outfit. 17, Cry off. 19, Orchid. 20, Unseeing. 22, Strolled. 24, Imbibe. 26, Great North Road.

Down: 1, Scenario writer. 2, Safe. 3, Tablet. 4, Proposer. 5, Stir. 7, Twitch. 8, Diary of a Nobody. 12, Match. 14, Rhone. 16, Indolent. 18, Murder. 21, Slight. 23, Oval. 25, Book.

PUZZLE No. 69

Across: 1, Call sign. 5, Street. 9, Maritime. 10, Solder. 12, Oven. 13, Chicken-run. 15, Place on record. 19, Screen version. 23, Leominster. 25, Fake. 28, Images. 29, Disorder. 30, Twenty. 31, Agnostic.

Down: 1, Common. 2, Large. 3, Seth. 4, Gumshoe. 6, Those. 7, Elder-down. 8, Threnody. 11, Scan. 14, Wage. 15, Personage. 16, One. 17, Evil. 18, Psalmist. 20, Vest. 21, Reeling. 22, Metric. 24, Inept. 26, Audit. 27, Solo.

PUZZLE No. 70

Across: 1, Speak French. 9, Air-base. 10, Closure. 11, Eli. 12, Spatial. 13, Pullets. 14, Moo. 15, Nacre. 17, Scorn. 18, Set-up. 20, Altar. 22, Dud. 24, Gradual. 25, Control. 26, Ash. 27, Reflect. 28, Amended. 29, Cat and mouse.

Down: 1, Stream of traffic. 2, Evasion. 3, Kneel. 4, Recipient. 5, Noodles. 6, Household drudge. 7, Hansom. 8, Person. 16, Charlatan. 18, Sugary. 19, Prudent. 21, Rondeau. 23, Delude. 25, Chasm.

PUZZLE No. 71

Across: 1, Depress. 5, Racial. 9, Cremate. 10, Gambler. 11, Age. 12, Rapscallion. 13, Mafia. 14, Godfather. 16, Browsings. 17, Music. 19, Assimilated. 22, Tea. 23, Confirm. 24, Palmist. 26, Severn. 27, Stagger.

Down: 1, Declaim. 2, Piece of nonsense. 3, Era. 4, Sheep. 5, Regicides. 6, Camel. 7, All-night sitting. 8, Kroner. 12, Roads. 14, Gentlemen. 15, Armed. 16, Branch. 18, Chatter. 20, Maine. 21, Tapes. 25, Lea.

PUZZLE No. 72

Across: 1, Peace-offering. 8, Anna. 9, Cap. 10, Pre-war. 11, Ecumenical. 13, Amin. 14, Leader. 16, Embodied. 19, Latticed. 22, Trance. 25, Chin. 26, Correspond. 27, Frieze. 28, Arc. 29, Arch. 30, Court of Appeal.

Down: 1, Panache. 2, Alarmed. 3, Eccentric. 4, Fop. 5, Expel. 6, Iceland. 7, Granite. 12, Cheddar. 15, Apt. 17, Buttercup. 18, Ian. 20, Amharic. 21, Tonneau. 23, Appease. 24, Cynical. 26, Chest. 28, Alf.

PUZZLE No. 73

Across: 6, Counterbalance. 9, Unison. 10, High time. 11, Smothers. 13, Invite. 15, Obtuse. 17, Chalet. 19, Ascent. 20, Twenties. 22, Mantilla. 24, Doctor. 26, Keep one's hand in.

Down: 1, Economy of scale. 2, Puss. 3, Stance. 4, Languish. 5, Fact. 7, Rehash. 8, Come to the point. 12, Tithe. 14, Valet. 16, Settling. 18, Straps. 21, Endear. 23, Type. 25, Code.

PUZZLE No. 74

Across: 1, Cranford. 5, Arrest. 9, Serenade. 10, Plight. 12, Nell. 13, Depreciate. 15, Field of battle. 19, In circulation. 23, Weightless. 25, Oman. 28, Banana. 29, Snappier. 30, Enlist. 31, Westward.

Down: 1, Casing. 2, April. 3, Find. 4, Redhead. 6, Relic. 7, Edgbaston. 8, Tottered. 11, Graf. 14, Bear. 15, Fictional. 16, Owl. 17, Avis. 18, Viewable. 20, Ugly. 21, Absence. 22, Ingrid. 24, Hangs. 26, Moira. 27, Spot.

PUZZLE No. 75

Across: 1, Stage-struck. 9, Primate. 10, Seaside. 11, Nut. 12, Awkward. 13, Auditor. 14, Elf. 15, Title. 17, Dunce. 18, Layer. 20, Optic. 22, Mum. 24, Oranges. 25, Comical. 26, Spa. 27, Aniline. 28, Dealing. 29, Exhaust pipe.
Down: 1, Stick of dynamite. 2, Adamant. 3, Emend. 4, Testament. 5, Unaided. 6, Knitting-machine. 7, Uptake. 8, Degree. 16, Trousseau. 18, Loofah. 19, Roguish. 21, Campari. 23, Malaga. 25, Cadet.

PUZZLE No. 76

Across: 1, Casuist. 5, Ash-can. 9, Roedean. 10, Trucker. 11, Imp. 12, Broad-minded. 13, Fungi. 14, Notorious. 16, Aspirates. 17, Fated. 19, Furthermore. 22, Own. 23, Control. 24, Sherbet. 26, Greedy. 27, Succeed.
Down: 1, Cardiff. 2, Sleeping partner. 3, Ice. 4, Tango. 5, Antidotes. 6, Houri. 7, Asked for trouble. 8, Prudes. 12, Briar (or Brier). 14, Naturally. 15, Rifle. 16, Affect. 18, Donated. 20, Horde. 21, Oasis. 25, Etc.

PUZZLE No. 77

Across: 1, Unmentionable. 8, Swan. 9, Gun. 10, Turnip. 11, Inevitable. 13, Atom. 14, Istria. 16, Trickled. 19, Japanese. 22, Runway. 25, Oslo. 26, Constantly. 27, Inform. 28, Cab. 29, Town. 30, Helicopter pad.
Down: 1, Unwinds. 2, Miniver. 3, Nightmare. 4, Ian. 5, Nitre. 6, Barrack. 7, Episode. 12, Bittern. 15, Tip. 17, Irritable. 18, Law. 20, Absinth. 21, Axolotl. 23, Non-stop. 24, Allowed. 26, Comic. 28, Cap.

PUZZLE No. 78

Across: 1, Customs union. 8, Abridge. 9, Chattel. 11, Transistor. 12, Ruin. 14, Reporter. 16, Miners. 17, Per. 19, Nested. 21, Vertebra. 24, Airy. 25, Encouraged. 27, Detract. 28, Moisten. 29, Cherry brandy.
Down: 1, Car lamp. 2, Side street. 3, Overstep. 4, Sector. 5, Near. 6, Obtrude. 7, Matter in hand. 10, Long-standing. 13, Distortion. 15, Rev. 18, Reformer. 20, Stretch. 22, Bigotry. 23, Knotty. 26, Pair.

PUZZLE No. 79

Across: 1, Hold your tongue. 9, Repeal. 10, Wine-skin. 11, Objector. 13, Anthem. 15, Ingrid. 17, Odious. 19, Advent. 20, Strangle. 22, Disperse. 24, Button. 26, Merchant seaman.
Down: 1, Three Blind Mice. 2, Blue. 3, Eyelet. 4, Standard. 5, Ants. 7, Upward. 8, Universal joint. 12, Eagle. 14, Thorn. 16, Internal. 18, Ascent. 21, Rubber. 23, Peck. 25, Tome.

PUZZLE No. 80

Across: 1, Midnight. 5, Swipes. 9, Seascape. 10, Redcar. 12, Idea. 13, Discretion. 15, Going straight. 19, Hurricane-lamp. 23, Subsidence. 25, Acre. 28, Malign. 29, Portrait. 30, Nailed. 31, Peep-show.
Down: 1, Mosaic. 2, Drake. 3, Inch. 4, Hopping. 6, Where. 7, Picking up. 8, Serenity. 11, Scot. 14, Gigi. 15, Garibaldi. 16, Sun. 17, Alan. 18, Chessman. 20, Aden. 21, Enclose. 22, Bestow. 24, Ingle. 26, Clash. 27, Stop.

PUZZLE No. 81

Across: 1, Call to order. 9, Trances. 10, Scuttle. 11, Tot. 12, Finance. 13, Ingress. 14, Eel. 15, Curia. 17, Tutor. 18, Scrap. 20, Sweet. 22, Tip. 24, Abstain. 25, Tempest. 26, Ado. 27, Stiffen. 28, Onerous. 29, Galley-slave.
Down: 1, Channel crossing. 2, Laconic. 3, Taste. 4, Obstinate. 5, Drugget. 6, Rotten to the core. 7, Stifle. 8, Censor. 16, Resonance. 18, Sparse. 19, Playful. 21, Tempera. 23, Potash. 25, Tools.

PUZZLE No. 82

Across: 5, Drowses. 5, String. 9, Chester. 10, Bouncer. 11, Ali. 12, Unguardedly. 13, Magog. 14, Heiresses. 16, Pleasance. 17, Scion. 19, Pretensions. 22, Cos. 23, Adoring. 24, Nipping. 26, Cygnet. 27, Regency.
Down: 1, Declaim. 2, Opening ceremony. 3, Set. 4, Shrug. 5, Submarine. 6, Round. 7, Nice distinction. 8, Troyes. 12, Urges. 14, Hindsight. 15, Eases. 16, Poplar. 18, Nosegay. 20, Evian. 21, Owner. 25, Pig.

PUZZLE No. 83

Across: 1, Chateaubriand. 8, Area. 9, Pie. 10, Glance. 11, Clodhopper. 13, Exit. 14, Agenda. 16, Exporter. 19, Reprieve. 22, Oncost. 25, Beef. 26, Dutch uncle. 27, Priest. 28, Bet. 29, Aide. 30, Watch and chain.
Down: 1, Cork-leg. 2, Abandon. 3, Espionage. 4, Use. 5, Roger. 6, Amateur. 7, Decline. 12, Present. 15, ESP. 17, Prophetic. 18, Two. 20, Eyebrow. 21, Reflect. 23, Cantata. 24, Saladin. 26, Ditch. 28, Ben.

PUZZLE No. 84

Across: 1, Conquistador. 8, Oranges. 9, Cranium. 11, Bridegroom. 12, Mien. 14, Nightcap. 16, Bounds. 17, Mam. 19, Torque. 21, Displace. 24, Onus. 25, Comicstrip. 27, Sailing. 28, Thinner. 29, Remonstrance.
Down: 1, Craving. 2, Neglectful. 3, Upstream. 4, Sector. 5, Alas. 6, Opinion. 7, Combinations. 10, Mine-sweepers. 13, Compassion. 15, Pad. 18, Minister. 20, Routine. 22, Arrange. 23, Forges. 26, Lino.

PUZZLE No. 85

Across: 6, It's a small world. 9, Thrive. 10, Benefice. 11, Openings. 13, Inhale. 15, Embark. 17, Charge. 19, Stress. 20, Lateness. 22, Carbolic. 24, Median. 26, Inconsiderable.
Down: 1, High speed train. 2, Asti. 3, Astern. 4, Clannish. 5, Golf. 7, Ambush. 8, Local newspaper. 12, Noble. 14, Heron. 16, Restless. 18, Placid. 21, Timbre. 23, Boon. 25, Dubs.

PUZZLE No. 86

Across: 1, Backward. 5, Statue. 9, Reprieve. 10, Gallop. 12, Nine. 13, Trade paper. 15, Nursery school. 19, Once upon a time. 23, Headstrong. 25, Able. 28, Animal. 29, Estimate. 30, Leered. 31, Marsh-gas.
Down: 1, Boring. 2, Capon. 3, Weir. 4, Reverse. 6, Tramp. 7, Telephone. 8, Expertly. 11, Eddy. 14, Urdu. 15, Nectarine. 16, Run. 17, Clip. 18, Moth-ball. 20, Ogre. 21, Amnesia. 22, Recess. 24, Slate. 26, Bhang. 27, Hiss.

PUZZLE No. 87

Across: 1, Parting shot. 9, Rubicon. 10, Dungeon. 11, Ell. 12, Olivier. 13, Intense. 14, Yet. 15, Taste. 17, Norse. 18, Crawl. 20, Noses. 22, Bag. 24, Assigns. 25, Compile. 26, Car. 27, Promote. 28, Arrears. 29, Time to spare.
Down: 1, Public transport. 2, Receipt. 3, Inner. 4, Godliness. 5, Honiton. 6, The Angry Brigade. 7, Priory. 8, Sneeze. 16, Senescent. 18, Clamps. 19, Lugworm. 21, Samaria. 23, Greasy. 25, Crass.

PUZZLE No. 88

Across: 1, Gallant. 5, Repack. 9, Outworn. 10, Dilemma. 11, Nil. 12, Accommodate. 13, Scene. 14, Pantheist. 16, Lightness. 17, Venus. 19, Transmitter. 22, One. 23, Endorse. 24, Astound. 26, Priest. 27, Pioneer.
Down: 1, Grounds. 2, Little Englander. 3, Ado. 4, Tonic. 5, Rudiments. 6, Polio. 7, Companion volume. 8, Patent. 12, Alert. 14, President. 15, Hover. 16, Litter. 18, Spender. 20, Spree. 21, Tramp. 25, Two.

PUZZLE No. 89

Across: 1, Millionairess. 8, Plan. 9, Pip. 10, Stella. 11, Inimitable. 13, Then. 14, Vernon. 16, Liberate. 19,

Eighteen. 22, Oracle. 25, Scum. 26, Prevention. 27, Pierce. 28, Sea. 29, Nail. 30, Excess baggage.
Down: 1, Melange. 2, Lineman. 3, Impotence. 4, Nap. 5, Issue. 6, Erector. 7, Solvent. 12, Balance. 15, Rug. 17, Boomerang. 18, Arc. 20, Incline. 21, Homeric. 23, Antonia. 24, Leonine. 26, Press. 28, Sob.

PUZZLE No. 90

Across: 1, Record player. 8, Alarmed. 9, Outcrop. 11, Extricates. 12, Semi. 14, Side-show. 16, Tic-tac. 17, Rat. 19, Author. 21, Register. 24, Item. 25, Concluding. 27, Lookout. 28, Inn sign. 29, Morning-glory.
Down: 1, Reacted. 2, Commission. 3, Radiator. 4, Plover. 5, Asti. 6, Earnest. 7, Waterspaniel. 10, Prince Regent. 13, Diminuendo. 15, War. 18, Teaching. 20, Tremolo. 22, Trinity. 23, Rotten. 26, Torn.

PUZZLE No. 91

Across: 6, Order of the Bath. 9, Wheeze. 10, Nightjar. 11, Organdie. 13, Elapse. 15, Uplift. 17, Angora. 19, Person. 20, Absentee. 22, Divinity. 24, Office. 26, Breathing-space.
Down: 1, Mother Superior. 2, Adze. 3, Friend. 4, Shagreen. 5, Abut. 7, Finger. 8, Transparencies. 12, Atlas. 14, Acorn. 16, Fanlight. 18, Banyan. 21, Scouse. 23, Iran. 25, Flat.

PUZZLE No. 92

Across: 1, Purchase. 5, Nimbus. 9, Pediment. 10, Deacon. 12, Noon. 13, Ventilator. 15, Dead man's chest. 19, Rickmansworth. 23, Baby-minder. 25, Scum. 28, Brainy. 29, Remedial. 30, Endure. 31, Psaltery.
Down: 1, Piping. 2, Radio. 3, Hemp. 4, Sunbeam. 6, Ideal. 7, Back teeth. 8, Sonority. 11, Stun. 14, Warm. 15, Duck-board. 16, Ass. 17, Cork. 18, Probable. 20, Nine. 21, Whereas. 22, Smelly. 24, Miner. 26, Clive. 27, Peel.

PUZZLE No. 93

Across: 1, Perfect fool. 9, Cripple. 10, Satisfy. 11, Cut. 12, Entreat. 13, Airport. 14, Doh. 15, Score. 17, Wiper. 18, Satyr. 20, Extra. 22, Rip. 24, Unwinds. 25, Recount. 26, Poe. 27, Formosa. 28, Arising. 29, Danger money.
Down: 1, Paint the town red. 2, Repress. 3, Erect. 4, Testament. 5, Outgrow. 6, Lost opportunity. 7, Screed. 8, Oyster. 16, Open space. 18, Stuffy. 19, Runcorn. 21, Auction. 23, Potage. 25, Realm.

PUZZLE No. 94

Across: 1, Lowland. 5, Warble. 9, Crackle. 10, Lighter. 11, Ugh. 12, Commandment. 13, Eerie. 14, Professor. 16, Stockport. 17, Tiffs. 19, Premonition. 22, Rio. 23, Realise. 24, Leander. 26, Street. 27, Treated.
Down: 1, Lecture. 2, Weather forecast. 3, Ark. 4, Dream. 5, Walkabout. 6, Raged. 7, Letters of credit. 8, Crater. 12, Check. 14, Prominent. 15, Eaten. 16, Superb. 18, Scoured. 20, Olive. 21, Islet. 25, Age.

PUZZLE No. 95

Across: 1, Kidderminster. 8, Snub. 9, Pot. 10, Trench. 11, Pastorally. 13, Rout. 14, Lesson. 16, Ultimate. 19, Stafford. 22, Nettle. 25, Vera. 26, Correction. 27, Waiter. 28, Bee. 29, Naif. 30, Lick into shape.
Down: 1, Kinsale. 2, Debates. 3, Esperanto. 4, Mat. 5, Natty. 6, Theorem. 7, Recruit. 12, Launder. 15, Spa. 17, Tenseness. 18, Aft. 20, Toe-nail. 21, Frantic. 23, Titania. 24, Leonine. 26, Corgi. 28, Bat.

PUZZLE No. 96

Across: 1, Strip cartoon. 8, Airline. 9, Thistle. 11, Playfellow. 12, Fret. 14, Interest. 16, Inform. 17, Saw. 19, Hogged. 21, Reversal. 24, Rile. 25, Appetising. 27, Station. 28, Oranges. 29, Chesterfield.
Down: 1, Servant. 2, Reinforced. 3, Peerless. 4, Action. 5, Thin. 6, Ontario. 7, Harpsichords. 10, Entomologist. 13, Indelicate. 15, Tar.

18, Werewolf. 20, Goliath. 22, Swigged. 23, Sponge. 26, Miss.

PUZZLE No. 97

Across: 6, Taking for a ride. 9, Aghast. 10, Engaging. 11, Scotched. 13, Manner. 15, Reside. 17, Animus. 19, Defers. 20, Round-arm. 22, Standard. 24, Lament. 26, Presence of mind.
Down: 1, Stage carpenter. 2, Skua. 3, Snatch. 4, Dragoman. 5, Drag. 7, Fiends. 8, Donkey Serenade. 12, Taste. 14, Named. 16, Disdains. 18, Bridge. 21, Uplift. 23, Nose. 25, Main.

PUZZLE No. 98

Across: 1, Platform. 5, Coffin. 9, Panorama. 10, Diving. 12, Else. 13, Intolerant. 15, Force the issue. 19, Railway engine. 23, Inhabitant. 25, Wake. 28, Afford. 29, Overlord. 30, Yellow. 31, Whistler.
Down: 1, Pepper. 2, Agnes. 3, Form. 4, Romance. 6, Olive. 7, Fricasse. 8, Nighties. 11, Pooh. 14, Crew. 15, Frightful. 16, Tee. 17, Iris. 18, Ordinary. 20, Yeti. 21, Nineveh. 22, Leader. 24, Burro. 26, Atoll. 27, Arms.

PUZZLE No. 99

Across: 1, Chicken-feed. 9, Airline. 10, Incense. 11, Egg. 12, Relates. 13, Healers. 14, Too. 15, Cairo. 17, Troon. 18, Mafia. 20, First. 22, Sip. 24, Neither. 25, Serious. 26, Mai. 27, Gondola. 28, Mourner. 29, Sheet-anchor.
Down: 1, Circle of friends. 2, Idiotic. 3, Knees. 4, Neighbour. 5, Enchant. 6, Dangerous corner. 7, Carrot. 8, Reason. 16, Informant. 18, Manage. 19, Athlone. 21, Through. 23, Pastry. 25, Simon.

PUZZLE No. 100

Across: 1, Orchard. 5, Damask. 9, Tuneful. 10, Saltash. 11, Ear. 12, Leatherhead. 13, Storm. 14, Erroneous. 16, Eightsome. 17, Paris. 19, Practically. 22, Ode. 23, Origins. 24, Blown up. 26, Eyelid. 27, Allayed.
Down: 1, Outlets. 2, Centre of gravity. 3, Alf. 4, Delta. 5, Discharge. 6, Molar. 7, Stage-door Johnny. 8, Shades. 12, Limit. 14, Exorcised. 15, Nippy. 16, Employ. 18, Steeped. 20, Twill. 21, Libya. 25, Owl.

PUZZLE No. 101

Across: 1, Fair and square. 8, Area. 9, Gem. 10, Instep. 11, Vacillates. 13, Note. 14, Amanda. 16, Mumblers. 19, Plangent. 22, Unable. 25, Twig. 26, Correction. 27, Priest. 28, Bar. 29, Nail. 30, Watering-place.
Down: 1, Forearm. 2, Italian. 3, Angel-cake. 4, Dam. 5, Quits. 6, Arsenal. 7, Erector. 12, Tempter. 15, Ada. 17, Mousetrap. 18, Ebb. 20, Low-brow. 21, Neglect. 23, Antenna. 24, Leonine. 26, Cater. 28, Ben.

PUZZLE No. 102

Across: 1, Depopulation. 8, Also-ran. 9, Granted. 11, Tarnishing. 12, Menu. 14, Abdullah. 16, Petrol. 17, Gas. 19, Mirage. 21, Scraping. 24, Stub. 25, Chinchilla. 27, Cadmium. 28, Imburse. 29, Friend in need.
Down: 1, Desired. 2, Persiflage. 3, Punch-bag. 4, Legend. 5, Trap. 6, Outwear. 7, Martial music. 10, Double-glazed. 13, Detachable. 15, Has. 18, Scansion. 20, Rounder. 22, Ill-bred. 23, Shamed. 26, Mine.

PUZZLE No. 103

Across: 6, Pop the question. 9, Matter. 10, Aircraft. 11, Mountain. 13, Defect. 15, Taoism. 17, Pelota. 19, Africa. 20, Interest. 22, Subsides. 24, Relict. 26, In the firm's time.
Down: 1, Speak out of turn. 2, Spot. 3, Sherpa. 4, Begrudge. 5, Stir. 7, Quaint. 8, Official secret. 12, Naomi. 14, Floor. 16, Stand-off. 18, Kisser. 21, Thrush. 23, Soho. 25, Laid.

PUZZLE No. 104

Across: 1, Gatepost. 5, Mascot. 9, Top-heavy. 10, Repast. 12, Etch. 13, Incidental. 15, Caught napping. 19, Discrepancies. 23, Peashooter. 25,

Cadi. 28, Ideals. 29, Flapjack. 30, Nestor. 31, Ascended.
Down: 1, Gather. 2, Topic. 3, Peel. 4, Seventh. 6, Adele. 7, Coat-tails. 8, Tutelage. 11, Lion. 14, Burr. 15, Castanets. 16, Tea. 17, Pain. 18, Adoption, 20, Plot. 21, Needles. 22, Wicked. 24, Hello. 26, Award. 27, Apse.

PUZZLE No. 105

Across: 1, Cuckoo-clock, 9, Airline. 10, Austere. 11, Rum. 12, Dolores. 13, Episode. 14, Ass. 15, Paste. 17, Gaffe. 18, Bedew. 20, Ionic. 22, Hub. 24, Whitlow. 25, Swinger. 26, Rye. 27, Aniline. 28, Niagara. 29, Gamekeepers.
Down: 1, Careless driving. 2, Chirrup. 3, Overs. 4, Chameleon. 5, Ousting. 6, Keep off the grass. 7, Sandra. 8, Severe. 16, Shipwreck. 18, Bowman. 19, William. 21, Climate. 23, Barman. 25, Sense.

PUZZLE No. 106

Across: 1, Custard. 5, Assume. 9, Raiment. 10, Scourge. 11, Ink. 12, Instructive. 13, Final. 14, Contender. 16, Expertise. 17, Doubt. 19, Chain-letter. 22, Rap. 23, Rotunda. 24, Present. 26, Fringe. 27, Dresser.
Down: 1, Cardiff. 2, Sticking-plaster. 3, Age. 4, Dates. 5, Assurance, 6, Stoic. 7, Married quarters. 8, Meteor. 12, Idler. 14, Crime wave, 15, Elder. 16, Escort. 18, Tapster. 20, Ninon. 21, Typed. 25, Eve.

PUZZLE No. 107

Across: 1, Traveller's joy. 8, Dish. 9, Asp. 10, Begone. 11, Pedestrian. 13, Lien. 14, Steele. 16, Mistress. 19, Bulletin. 22, Ironic. 25, Diva. 26, Sweetheart. 27, Winner. 28, Owl. 29, Aran. 30, German measles.
Down: 1, Trident. 2, Athlete. 3, Enactment. 4, Lip. 5, Robin. 6, Juggler. 7, Yankees. 12, Immense. 15, Eel. 17, Scintilla. 18, Eon. 20, Uniting. 21, Learner. 23, Overall. 24, Inroads. 26, Syria. 28, Ohm..

PUZZLE No. 108

Across: 1, Decoratively. 8, Havanas. 9, Licence. 11, Misleading. 12, Alec. 14, Insolent. 16, Brenda. 17, Top. 19, Nylons. 21, Watch-dog. 24, Huge. 25, Southerner. 27, Pitcher. 28, Clement. 29, French lesson.
Down: 1, Devises. 2, Concealing. 3, Resident. 4, Talent. 5, Vice. 6, Lanolin. 7, Championship. 10, Exchange rate. 13, Cricketers. 15, Tow. 18, Pastiche. 20, Lighter. 22, Dungeon. 23, Fourth. 26, Chin.

PUZZLE No. 109

Across: 6, House of Commons. 9, Census. 10, Toilsome. 11, Accurate. 13, Import. 15, Notice. 17, Heroic. 19, Attain. 20, Airedale. 22, Aberdeen. 24, Bowery. 26, Devil's advocate.
Down: 1, Chief Constable. 2, Fuss. 3, Persia. 4, Positive. 5, Amps. 7, Fatten. 8, Numerical order. 12, Ultra. 14, Proud. 16, Converse. 18, Pained. 21, Ribbon. 23, Rain. 25, Wear.

PUZZLE No. 110

Across: 1, Mandrill. 5, Big top. 9, Postcard. 10, Office. 12, Isle. 13, Playwright. 15, Cousins-german. 19, Improbability. 23, Corybantic. 25, Scar. 28, Urgent. 29, Mandolin. 30, Tittle. 31, Leanings.
Down: 1, Maplin. 2, Nasal. 3, Rack. 4, Lorelei. 6, Infer. 7, Thingummy. 8, Pleating. 11, Ayes. 14, Ludo. 15, Copyright. 16, Nab. 17, Exit. 18, Discount. 20, Aunt. 21, Imitate. 22, Brands. 24, Banal. 26, Colin. 27, Odin.

PUZZLE No. 111

Across: 1, Bolt upright. 9, Grumble. 10, Verbose. 11, Rue. 12, Insults. 13, Run-down . 14, Ell. 15, Ashen. 17, Elder. 18, Desks. 20, Sweat. 22, One. 24, Gorilla. 25, Screech. 26, Not. 27, Spurned. 28, Anagram. 29, See eye to eye.
Down: 1, Brussels sprouts. 2, Lobelia. 3, Users. 4, Reverence. 5, Garonne. 6, Too good to be true. 7, Ignite. 8, Tenner. 16, Husbandry. 18, Digest.

19, Silence. 21, Terrace. 23. Exhume. 25, Start.

PUZZLE No. 112

Across: 1, Sackbut. 5, Reason. 9, Regency. 10, Palette. 11, Air. 12, Bitter Sweet. 13, Title. 14, Prescribe. 16, Greatcoat. 17, Aches. 19, Prohibitive. 22, Lad. 23, Endorse. 24, Satanic. 26, Prosit. 27, Exposed.
Down: 1, Servant. 2, Cigarette-holder. 3, Bun. 4, Tryst. 5, Represent. 6, Atlas. 7, On the right lines. 8, Kettle. 12, Bleat. 14, Prominent. 15, Chase. 16, Gopher. 18, Seduced. 20, Idris. 21, Issue. 25, Tip.

PUZZLE No.113

Across: 1, Volume control. 8, Gown. 9, Urn. 10, Trance. 11, Delightful. 13, Iron. 14, Stigma. 16, Elongate. 19, Sketches. 22, Exempt. 25, Form. 26, Classified. 27, Chalet. 28, Ape. 29, Note. 30, Warm reception.
Down: 1, Violent. 2, Landing. 3, Mouth-wash. 4, Can. 5, Natal. 6, Reading. 7, Lock out. 12, Freesia. 15, Ike. 17, Oversleep. 18, Arm. 20, Know-how. 21, Tumbler. 23, Effendi. 24, Preston. 26, Cater. 28, Arc.

PUZZLE No. 114

Across: 1, Semicircular. 8, Opinion. 9, Clipper. 11, Prosecutor. 12, Arid. 14, Offended. 16, Bowler. 17, Doh. 19, Income. 21, Geranium. 24, Iota. 25, Definition. 27, Gorilla. 28, Agitate. 29, Metal fatigue.
Down: 1, Spin-off. 2, Maiden name. 3, Consumed. 4, Rector. 5, Unit. 6, Apparel. 7, Compromising. 10, Rude reminder. 13, Polarising. 15, Dog. 18, Hesitant. 20, Coterie. 22, Imitate. 23, Behalf. 26, Plea.

PUZZLE No. 115

Across: 6, Hot water bottle. 9, Adored. 10, Conforms. 11, Swindler. 13, Oblate. 15, Intact. 17, Ascend. 19, Middle. 20, Aversion. 22, Stiletto. 24, Choppy. 26, Bristol fashion.
Down: 1, Shadow minister. 2, Stir. 3, Handel. 4, Abandons. 5, Otto. 7, Escort. 8, Limited company. 12, Noted. 14, Leeds. 16, Creation. 18, Pay-off. 21, Excise. 23, Last. 25, Omit.

PUZZLE No. 116

Across: 1, Bird-lime. 5, Dispel. 9, Seminary. 10, Secret. 12, Lane. 13, Interloper. 15, Dark Continent. 19, Home Secretary. 23, Penicillin. 25, Stir. 28, Owners. 29, Becoming. 30, Keeper. 31, Startled.
Down: 1, Basalt. 2, Roman. 3, Link. 4, Moronic. 6, Ideal. 7, Periphery. 8, Literate. 11, Bean. 14, Arms. 15, Dominance. 16, Oar. 17, Iraq. 18, Chapbook. 20, Cell. 21, Exigent. 22, Frigid. 24, Curve. 26, Twill. 27, Poor.

PUZZLE No.117

Across: 1, Challenging. 9, Unnerve. 10, Vintner. 11, Gee. 12, Anemone. 13, Literal. 14, Yob. 15, Tacit. 17, Dally. 18, Paris. 20, Swear. 22, Sob. 24, Petunia. 25, Austere. 26, Nag. 27, Related. 28, Notable. 29, Serial story.
Down: 1, Canterbury Tales. 2, Airport. 3, Liege. 4, Novelette. 5, Ignited. 6, General Assembly. 7, Queasy. 8, Brolly. 16, Cassandra. 18, Pipers. 19, Senator. 21, Risotto. 23, Brevet. 25, Agnes.

PUZZLE No. 118

Across: 1, Papoose. 5, Expect. 9, Trotter. 10, Flounce. 11, Fur. 12, Theological. 13, Loser. 14, President. 16, Price list. 17, Excel. 19, Traditional. 22, Mow. 23, Emirate. 24, Robinia. 26, Sneeze. 27, Essayed.
Down: 1, Pitiful. 2, Procrastination. 3, Out. 4, Eerie. 5, Effulgent. 6, Prong. 7, Conscience money. 8, Pellet. 12, Three. 14, Privilege. 15, Ideal. 16, Putter. 18, Lowland. 20, Inane. 21, Nurse. 25, Bus.

PUZZLE No. 119

Across: 1, Pale imitation. 8, Inca. 9, Sin. 10, Sleepy. 11, Lighterman. 13, Irun. 14, Regret. 16, Chuckles. 19,

Concorde. 22, Nectar. 25, Item. 26, Chesterton. 27, Amulet. 28, Bar. 29, Also. 30, Mixed feelings.
Down: 1, Pantile. 2, Leather. 3, Inspector. 4, Inn. 5, Arson. 6, Ice-rink. 7, Neptune. 12, Machete. 15, Gun. 17, Unnatural. 18, Lot. 20, Optimum. 21, Complex. 23, Certain. 24, Arouses. 26, Cited. 28, Bee.